Ann Ladbury's Book of Dressmaking

ANN LADBURY'S BOOK OF DRESSMAKING

This edition specially produced for
members of the Ann Ladbury Dressmaking Club

by Ann Ladbury

LEONARD HILL BOOKS
LONDON: 1970

An Intertext Publisher

ISBN 0 249 44016 4

First published by
Leonard Hill Books
a division of
International Textbook Company Limited
158 Buckingham Palace Road, London SW1

Printed by Butler & Tanner Ltd,
Frome and London

Dear Club Member,

I am very pleased that Ann Ladbury has been able to arrange for a Club edition of this book, for I am sure that it will quickly become an invaluable guide and aid for all dressmakers.

This is Ann's first book and there is a promise of further books to come.

As President I would like to welcome you as a member, and express the hope that you will enjoy to the full your dressmaking and the facilities which the Club will offer.

Henry Marshall

DEAR CLUB MEMBER

This book has, to a large extent, been created by its potential readers. Over the past few years it has been my pleasure to answer a wide range of dressmaking problems following my lectures and my television programmes. These were put to me both by students and home dressmakers and it became obvious that there were many dressmakers who would welcome a practical reference book to which they could turn for guidance when faced with a sewing problem. This book has been written to meet their need.

The information given is arranged alphabetically both to facilitate quick, easy reference and to enable the book to be used whilst actually working on a garment. Detailed instructions are given to help beginners form a good groundwork but more advanced guidance is also presented for the experienced dressmaker.

Although primarily intended as a practical reference book theoretical aspects have not been neglected as these will be necessary to students following a formal course.

May I welcome you as a Club member and hope you enjoy all the facilities offered.

In conclusion I would particularly like to thank Beryl Rouse for doing the original drawings for the book.

Acknowledgements and thanks are also due to the following companies who supplied information and illustrations: J & P Coats Ltd, the Bogod Machine Co. Ltd, British Alcozip Ltd, Selectus Ltd, and W Whiteley Ltd for supplying photographs.

Ann Ladbury

LIST OF PHOTOGRAPHS

THE METRIC SYSTEM

All measurements in this book are given in British units with their metric equivalents in brackets, to help the student to familiarise herself with the metric system. In sewing one can only work to approximate amounts because, with very small operations like hand stitches and seam widths, so much depends on the fabric being handled and the skill of the worker. For this reason the metric equivalents are only taken to the nearest millimetre.

The scale below illustrates how a quick conversion can be made (1 inch equals approximately $2\frac{1}{2}$ (2·5) centimetres).

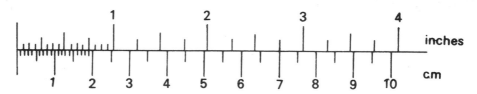

A

ACETATE

A cellulose fibre made from wood-pulp or cotton waste (cotton fibres too short to use for cotton fabrics). The fibre is made into a wide variety of fabrics for clothes and furnishings, including brocade, satin and taffeta, and it blends well with other fibres, particularly viscose rayon.

Acetate fabrics fray easily and may pull away at the seams after hard wear or if the garment is too tight, but they are not too difficult to handle. Most of them wash well by hand or machine, but care should be taken to crease these fabrics as little as possible during washing as the creases can easily become cracks in the fibre which are permanent. Garments should not be rolled up damp for the same reason.

ACRYLIC FIBRES

These include Acrilan and Courtelle which are made in the United Kingdom, and Dralon, Dynel, Crylor, Orlon, Creslan and Zefran which are made in other countries. Teklan, a moda-crylic fibre, is made into a range of flame-resistant fabrics. Acrylic fibres may be woven into a variety of fabrics including crêpe, jersey, blankets, knitwear, fur and fleecy fabrics. Mixtures of other fibres such as wool with acrylics combine the best qualities of each.

Acrylics wash well, provided they are not allowed to become too dirty and the washing instructions are followed, and they are easy to sew. Use synthetic thread with a fine machine needle and a No. 8 or 9 hand-sewing needle. Some of the woven materials tend to fray badly so allowance should be made for this when cutting out and handling.

ARROWHEADS

A decorative feature which also strengthens, the arrowhead (or Sprat's head) may be used at the tops of pleats and at the ends of bound pockets. Work them using buttonhole thread or

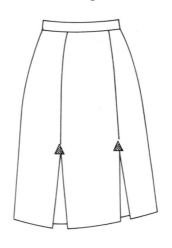

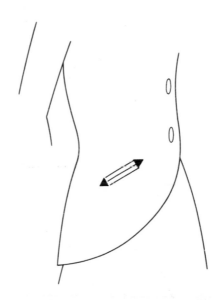

a fine crochet cotton. If the fabric is loosely woven or very light in weight place a small square of tape or lining behind the arrowhead and work through it. Begin by marking out a triangle with sharp tailor's chalk or small tackings. Tacks should match the colour of the material as they may be difficult to remove later.

1

ARROWHEADS

Use single thread and stab the needle through the work or the stitches may pucker the material.

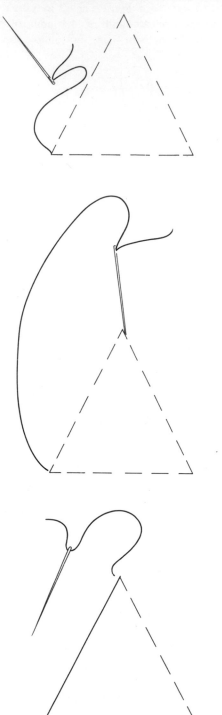
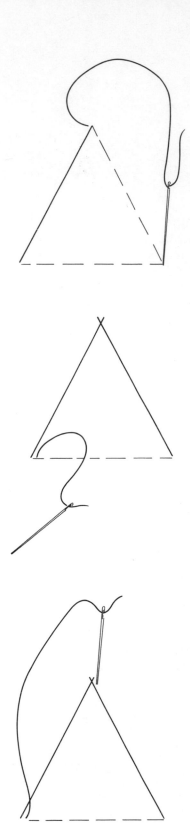

BALANCE MARKS

These are marks on the pattern which indicate where one piece of fabric is to be joined to another. On printed patterns they are often shown as black triangles or diamonds and may also be numbered. Some balance marks on straightforward seams can be disregarded by the experienced sewer but they are a useful guide on curved or shaped seams, for setting-in sleeves, for placing gathers and tucks, for complicated styles and where whole sections are cut on the cross and so liable to go out of shape. It should

B

BACKSTITCH

A full backstitch is used mainly for embroidery but a half backstitch is a useful strong stitch for small sections of work which are difficult to reach by machine. Use double thread if extra strength is required. The stitch should be as short as possible and pulled fairly tight. The stitch may be used for sewing in sleeves in woollens and soft fabrics (see *Sleeves*).

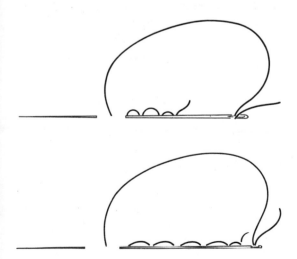

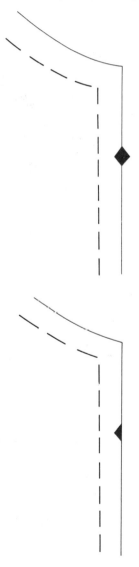

be remembered that an alteration when fitting can render the balance marks inaccurate (see *Fitting*).

Marking Balance Marks
Never cut balance marks inwards when cutting round the pattern as it weakens the turnings, and to cut them outwards from the pattern is rather time consuming.

It is more satisfactory to mark them either with tracing paper on the wrong side of the fabric or to place single tailor tacks in position across the turnings. Balance marks are more useful if they are marked both in the turning and over the fitting line as shown.

BAR TACK
1. *To Strengthen*
A strengthening tack put at the top of pleats and the end of openings, and worked on the wrong side where possible. Make a base of four or five stitches about $\frac{1}{8}''$ (4 mm) long and then cover them with loopstitch, picking up fabric as well as threads.

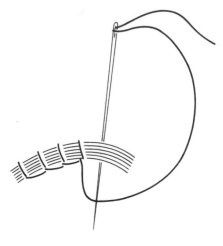

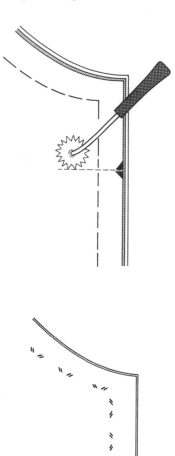

2. *Lining Bar Tack*
This tack is used to hold the hem of a coat lining loosely in position and also to hold the seams of lining in place in dresses and skirts. Pin the hem of the finished coat lining in position and work the tack under the edge. They are normally placed at seams so that they may be sewn on to

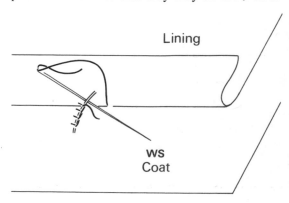

Lining

WS
Coat

double material. Work several strands of double thread, leaving them about $\frac{1}{2}''$ (15 mm) long, and then loopstitch them together. If a dress is made with a loose lining $\frac{1}{2}''$ (15 mm) bar tacks may be worked at intervals down the side seams to hold the lining in position.

An alternative method of making the tack is to use chain stitch.

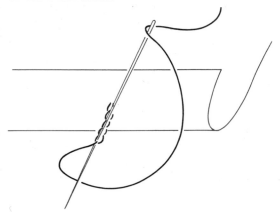

BASIC PATTERNS

Pattern companies make a range called Basic Patterns. These are plain styles without the addition of collars, cuffs, pleats, etc. Their purpose is to provide a basis for discovering where the figure deviates from normal. To do this the pattern is made up in sheeting or something similar (an old sheet is perfect) and tried on. All alterations are made on this and marked, and later transferred to other paper patterns as they are used. The basic pattern itself also provides a useful plain dress pattern to be made up in various fabrics.

BASTING

This stitch is used for joining pieces of material which are then to be handled as one fabric. The stitch varies in size between $\frac{1}{2}''$ (15 mm) and $2''$ (5 cm), depending upon the type of fabric being used and upon the size of the pieces. It is used for keeping interfacing in position on collars, openings, coat fronts, for holding lining in position and for securing pleats.

The stitch is normally worked flat on the table, using the forefinger of the left hand to help the fabric on to the needle with each stitch. Where layers of canvas are held together for putting into coats the stitches are not removed, but in all other cases they are removed when the garment is complete. Use tacking thread, begin with a knot and end with one back stitch.

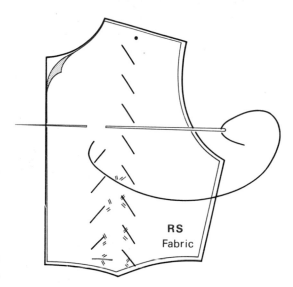

RS
Fabric

A smaller version called pad stitch is used for joining the interfacing to the under-collar for coats, etc. (*see Pad Stitch*).

Machine-basting is a large machine stitch which may be used on some fabrics in place of tacking for straight seams.

BELT LOOPS AND CARRIERS

Loops should be wider than the belt, and if the ends are not caught in the seam then the back of the fabric should be reinforced with a piece of interfacing or tape.

1. *Thread Loops*

Place the belt in position and pin, then using double thread make several strands across the belt. Remove the belt and work loopstitch over the strands, keeping the stitches as close as possible.

5

2. *Fabric Loop in a Seam*

This loop is put in before the seam is made.

Cut a piece of material on the straight grain $\frac{1}{2}''-\frac{3}{4}''$ (15–20 mm) wide and fold it lengthwise with right sides together. Machine $\frac{1}{4}''$ (8 mm) from the raw edges and turn it through with a bodkin. Tack the edge and press it. Place the loop in position on the right side of the section of garment so that the ends overlap the fitting line by $\frac{1}{4}''$ (8 mm). Place the second piece of garment in position and make the seam in the usual way, but work two rows of machining across the belt loop. This type of loop cannot be inserted into a french or fell seam.

3. *Stitched Fabric Loop*

These are often used on heavy cotton materials such as denim and sailcloth, and made conspicuous by outside machining, but they may be attached by hand.

Cut the material on the straight grain about $1''$ (2·5 cm) wide and at least $1''$ longer than the width of the belt. Turn in each side $\frac{1}{4}''$ (8 mm) and fold again. Tack and press before machining both edges. Turn in $\frac{1}{4}''$ (8 mm) at each end and trim off the corners as shown. At this stage the loop

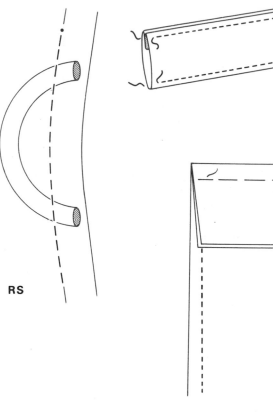

RS

WS

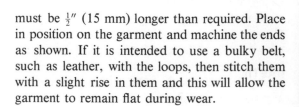

must be $\frac{1}{2}''$ (15 mm) longer than required. Place in position on the garment and machine the ends as shown. If it is intended to use a bulky belt, such as leather, with the loops, then stitch them with a slight rise in them and this will allow the garment to remain flat during wear.

6

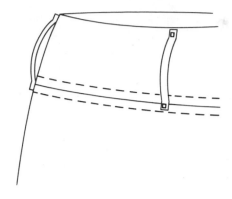

BELTS

1. *Tie Belts*

Soft tie belts can be made to any width by folding in half a strip of fabric cut on the straight or cross grain, and starting at the centre of the strip pin vertically, checking that the grain is not pulled out of place. Tack and then machine the belt in two sections, starting near the centre and stitching the length of the belt, and across the ends. Leave a gap of about 3″ (8 cm) at the centre as shown to turn the belt through. A slightly crisp belt can be achieved by making up with a layer of organdie inside.

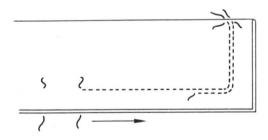

For neat ends: To make sure pointed ends are the same shape cut a template and tack or chalk round it. Work one stitch across the corners, and in the point itself make the final stitch straight as shown. If the fabric is loosely woven or inclined to fray, machine the ends a second time. Trim off all turnings in the corners and points.

Turn the belt through, using a knitting needle, and roll and tack the edge carefully. Close the gap by slip-stitching and press the belt.

A very narrow belt is sometimes difficult to turn through, so tack it with a piece of tape or strong thread inside. Machine the long side and then stitch across one end to secure the tape. Pull the belt through using the tape. With this method the ends have to be neatened after turning, but they may be covered with a Chinese ball button or the raw edge can be tucked inside and neatly pulled together with a gathering thread.

Cord can be inserted in this belt by stitching a length of cord to the end of the tape before pulling through.

2. *Stiffened Belts*

Use petersham (shrink first), bonded interfacing, buckram, stiffened cotton or belt-backing for stiffening and begin by cutting it exactly to the length and width required, and shape the ends. Cut a piece of fabric on the straight grain longer than needed and a random width (or at least three times the width of the backing). Place the belt-backing in position and tack it in position or iron it on if it is adhesive. Paper-backed

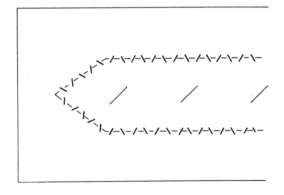

Bondina Fusible Fleece can be used to attach non-adhesive backings. If the heat of the iron is liable to damage the fabric, cover the work with a damp cloth or with paper. Other backings are attached all round with catch stitch. Fold the fabric on to the backing and tack a little way from the edge, fixing pointed corners by mitring the fabric. Tack one side of the fabric to the centre of the backing, trim away all surplus fabric and fold under the second side of fabric. Hem this to the centre of the belt and hem the ends. Finish belt by edge-stitching from the right side if desired.

BIAS

The term bias (bias-cut; on the bias, etc.) usually refers to any edge of material which is cut off the straight thread. True bias (or true cross) refers to an edge running at exactly 45° to the straight

thread. The latter has a maximum amount of stretch, and pieces cut at angles less than 45° will stretch proportionately less. These qualities are considered when using bias fabric to finish edges (see *Binding*) and also when cutting whole pattern pieces on the bias.

BINDING

A neat method of finishing an edge which shows equally on both sides and is decorative. It is used on shaped and straight edges and is normally made as narrow as the fabric will allow. Attractive results can be achieved by using plain and patterned fabrics and contrasting colours in all types of fabric, both thick and thin.

The binding itself is cut on the cross of the fabric as this will allow it to stretch and so fit snugly around shaped edges.

1. *Cutting*

For maximum stretch the bindings are cut on the true bias, that is, with the fabric folded so that the warp and weft threads are at right angles to each other. Cut the strips parallel to the fold, using a marker or tape measure. They are easier

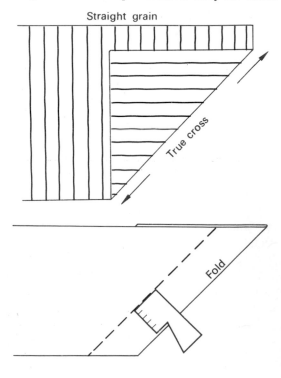

Straight grain

True cross

Fold

to cut if the fold is lightly pressed first. Pins will tend to pucker the material. The edges will not fray, so small turnings of $\frac{1}{4}''$ (8 mm) can be allowed.

Bias strips can also be cut from fabric not quite on the true cross provided it is not checked material. They will have less stretch but are adequate for straight edges or slightly shaped edges.

TO CALCULATE THE WIDTH

    (a)   Single bind = twice the finished width plus two turnings.

    (b)   Double bind = four times finished width plus two turnings.

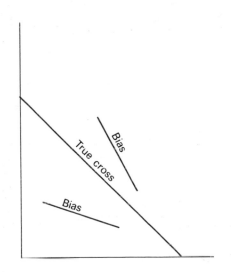

2. *Stretching*

To prevent puckering on the finished bind it helps to stretch the binding before applying it. Pin one end of the strip to the ironing board, stretch it slightly and pin the other end down. Press lightly with a damp cloth and leave it to cool before un-pinning. If the binding is to be used around a very sharp curve, then shape it slightly as you stretch it.

3. *Joining*

The ends of crossways strips are on the straight grain—if they have been cut from odd scraps of

fabric, then trim the ends off on the grain. The join must be made on the straight grain or the binding will not lie flat. Press a $\frac{1}{4}''$ (8 mm) turning to the wrong side on the ends to be joined. Place the ends close together to form a straight strip, lift the turnings and pin the two creases together, then tack and machine. Press the row of machining, press the join open and then trim the turnings.

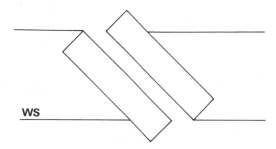

WS

4. *Applying Binding*

(a) SINGLE BIND

Place right side of strip to right side of garment, taking a $\frac{1}{4}''$ (8 mm) turning on the binding and placing it against the fitting line on the garment. The binding is easier to handle if the turning on the garment is left wider than that of the binding at this stage. Stretch the binding slightly around concave curves and ease it around convex curves. Use small tackings and no pins. Machine in place from the binding side as it tends to curl up, and use a small machine stitch.

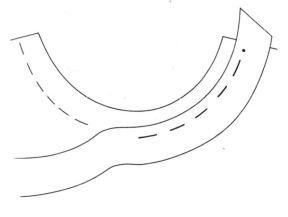

Press the row of machining after removing tackings and then trim the turnings to the exact width the binding is to be when finished. Do not layer the turnings or cut too much away as the turnings should fill the bind to make it plump.

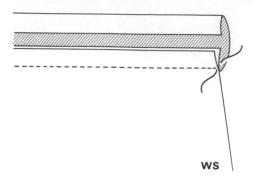

WS

Fold the raw edge down to meet the edge of the turnings, fold again and hem into the machine stitches. When hemming, put the needle into the fold following the straight grain on the binding or puckering may occur.

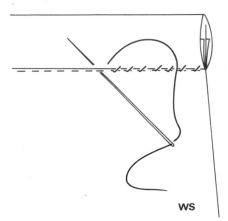

WS

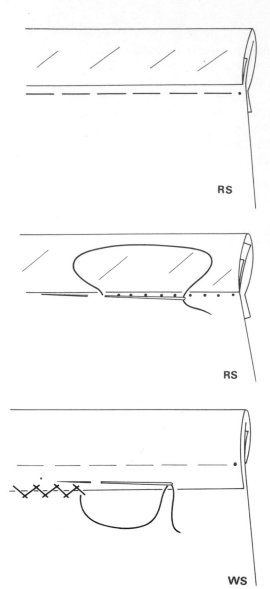

RS

RS

WS

NOTE: Binding with woollens and thick fabrics. Cut and apply the strips in the usual way, and trim the turnings to the correct width. Roll the binding to the wrong side and tack, working from the right side, just below the join. Work a back-stitch along the join, still working from the right side, and then finish off the binding on the wrong side by working herringbone stitch over the edge.

(*b*) DOUBLE BIND

This method is easier with fine fabrics such as chiffon, silk and lawn, as the width can be kept to a minimum and it gives a firm edge to the garment.

Fold the crossway strips in half and tack, but do not press as the fold line is not established until later. Place this against the fitting line and

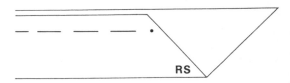

RS

attach in the usual way. After trimming, turn the fold to the wrong side, tack in position and hem the fold to the machine stitches. It will be seen that accuracy is essential with this method as the width of the finished bind cannot be altered after stitching.

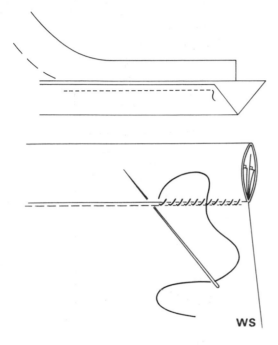

NOTE: Single and double binding may be applied to the wrong side of the work and then folded over on to the right side to be finished by a row of machining in the case of cottons, etc., or perhaps by a decorative stitch such as pin-stitch or feather-stitch on fine fabrics. With this method the binding is pulled down to cover the original row of machining.

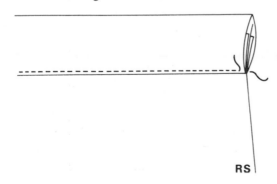

BONDED FABRICS

There are two main types of fabric that are referred to as bonded. The first is more correctly termed non-woven and includes interfacings such as those in the Vilene range, 'paper' fabrics and felt. In other words, all fabrics that are made by bonding fibres together instead of weaving. There is no straight of grain to check when cutting out and they do not fray, but the fabrics are not strong and are suitable only for loose styles which avoid strain, and short-life garments.

Many fabrics are now bonded or stuck to a backing material (usually jersey nylon) and some also have a layer of synthetic foam in between. The process is known as 'coin bonding', and obviates the necessity for lining or mounting the garment. They are referred to as bonded lace, bonded wool, etc. They should be sewn according to the outer fabric, although of course iron temperatures must be checked before pressing on the wrong side.

BROCADES—to handle

Brocades may be made from silk or rayon, and furnishing brocade is made from linen or rayon. Dress brocades may also contain metallic threads. These fabrics fray badly and require careful pressing, so the following hints may be useful.

1. Fit the pattern carefully before cutting out to lessen the amount of handling in making up. The lining could be cut out and fitted too before cutting the brocade.

2. When cutting out leave a little extra turning and immediately neaten the seam edges by overcasting or by using a zig-zag stitch on the machine.

3. Stay-stitch curved edges to prevent stretching. If the garment is to be mounted on a lining then do this before stay-stitching.

4. Use organdie, net or nylon organza to interface lightweight brocades and a thin bonded interfacing with heavy ones.

5. Use a fine machine needle and about 15–20 stitches to 1″ (2·5 cm) (to help prevent seams fraying out).

6. Use a number 8 or 9 hand-sewing needle.

7. Make open seams and neaten by machine or by binding with net.

8. Do not split darts open, avoid top stitching and make bound buttonholes, backing the fastening area and the buttonhole patch with a lightweight iron-on interfacing (the paper-backed variety is suitable).

9. Press brocades on the wrong side only, using the toe of a cool iron and no moisture. Those brocades containing metal threads (which are plastic coated) are easily cracked and this produces a permanent crease, so it is best to open seams with the fingers only and leave pressing with the iron until the garment is finished.

BUST DART

Shaping for the bust is provided by a dart which runs from the outer edge of the pattern piece towards the bust. The pocket of fullness made by the dart should fit comfortably over the bust. Pin out the dart on the pattern and check the position and size of the bust shaping. Small alterations are easy to make and can make all the difference to the fit and appearance of the garment. The size of the dart (that is, the width at the base), the length to its point, and the direction of the dart may be altered on the pattern, or even, if the alteration is small, in the fabric after the first fitting.

Alterations to Bust Dart

1. INCREASE IN SIZE. At the base of the dart take up an extra $\frac{1}{8}''$ (4 mm) each side and stitch the dart to the original point. NOTE: If the pocket produced in the fabric appears too big for the bust then reduce the width at the base.

2. INCREASE IN LENGTH. Mark a new point nearer to the bust point but still in line with the existing dart. Sew the dart from the original base points but run the stitching to the new point.

3. CHANGE IN DIRECTION. Mark a new point either above or below the existing dart point and, using the original base points, stitch the dart in the new position. NOTE: The maximum amount this point should be moved is about $\frac{3}{4}''$ (20 mm). If a greater adjustment than this is necessary it involves moving the whole dart and this comes under pattern alterations.

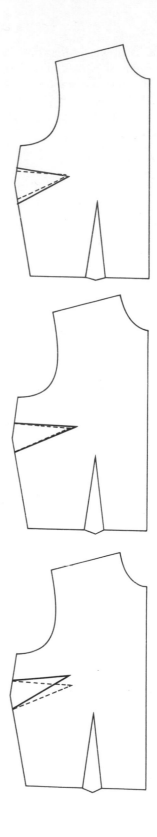

BUTTONS

1. *Choice*

Choose the size carefully according to the garment, the position and the size of the extension on the pattern allowed beyond the buttonhole position. For example, on a blouse there may only be $\frac{1}{2}''-\frac{3}{4}''$ (15–20 mm) extending beyond the centre front, so a small button is required that will not overlap the edge when it is fastened. A coat normally has $1''$ (2·5 cm) or more beyond the centre front line, so allowing for a larger button. Dome-shaped buttons have a slight shank under them, but they tend to wobble when used with thin fabrics. Holed buttons must have a thread shank made.

2. *Sewing on*

Sew through two layers of fabric plus a layer of interfacing and with woollens place a strip of linen in place as well. Use double thread and begin with a knot on thick fabrics. Wax the thread with beeswax for use on coats, jackets, woollen dresses, etc., as this will strengthen the thread. It will also help to keep the two threads together while sewing. Run the thread through beeswax two or three times and then twist the thread between the palms, winding the twisted section around the thumb while proceeding to the next section. This will make a strong cord like thread.

Work two back stitches to begin and then thread the button on to the needle. Push the needle in and out of the fabric in one movement, taking the stitch right through all layers of fabric.

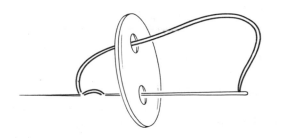

The length of the shank left must equal the thickness of the material to be fastened over it, that is, two layers of fabric and one layer of interfacing, so with a thick tweed the shank may have to be $\frac{1}{2}''$ (15 mm) long. It is not usually sufficient to sew the button on over a matchstick as this will only provide a shank of $\frac{1}{8}''$ (4 mm) or less. Work plenty of threads through the button and then wind the thread around the shank firmly to cover it. Finally pass the needle through to the wrong side and work a few firm stitches to fasten off. With lightweight or smooth fabrics it gives a neat finish to work loopstitch over the threads on the wrong side.

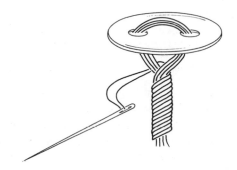

BUTTONHOLES

General Instructions

1. All types of buttonhole should be made through two layers of fabric plus a layer of interfacing, and many fabrics need further reinforcement in the form of a piece of linen or strong cotton. With fabrics that fray easily, add a piece of lightweight iron-on Vilene or Bondina Fusible Fleece to make handling easier.

2. POSITION. Button and buttonhole fastenings should only be used where there is sufficient overlap, and enough ease in the garment to ensure that the opening does not gape. The buttonholes should not be too near the edge of the wrap (see MARKING, below) and it is best to plan a minimum number needed to fasten the opening efficiently. The exact number depends upon the size of the button, the type of garment and the fabric. They should lie on the straight grain unless this is made impossible by the style.

3. DIRECTION. Where possible the buttonhole should lie in the direction of the strain—for example, horizontally on a blouse or dress front and along the length of a cuff or waistband—the exceptions to this are where the button and buttonhole is part of a style feature or where they are placed centrally on a strap opening, or on a loose-fitting garment in a lightweight fabric such as a chiffon blouse or a poplin shirt.

4. SIZE. The buttonhole should be slightly larger than the button, to allow easy fastening and to prevent undue wear, but some types of buttonhole give a little in use. Allowances for the thickness of the button should also be added to the length of the buttonhole. Amount of ease to be added:

(a)	Hand-worked	$\frac{1}{16}''$	(2 mm).
(b)	Machine-made	$\frac{1}{4}''$	(8 mm).
(c)	Bound	$\frac{1}{8}''$	(4 mm).
(d)	Piped	$\frac{1}{4}''$	(8 mm).

5. MARKING THE POSITION. The position of the buttonholes may be transferred from the paper pattern, but if any alterations have been made they may have to be re-spaced. Vertical buttonholes lie on the centre front line of a front opening, and horizontal buttonholes begin at the centre front (or a little beyond in thick fabrics) and extend back into the main part of the garment. In any case the buttonhole should be no closer to the edge than the diameter of the button so that when fastened the button does not extend over the edge.

Begin by marking the position of the end of the buttonholes (with chalk or tacking) and then make another mark to show the other end. Finally space and mark the buttonholes themselves.

Types of Buttonhole
  (a) Hand-worked.
  (b) Bound.
  (c) Piped.
  (d) Machine-made.

Method of making Hand-worked Buttonholes
1. Allow sufficient time to work all buttonholes at once to ensure an even tension is developed on the stitch (see *Hand Sewing*).

2. Baste around each marked buttonhole to hold all layers together.

3. Prepare a needle with single thread and a knot in the end (may be cut off later). Use sewing thread on all medium and lightweight fabrics, buttonhole twist on thicker fabrics.

4. Cut the first buttonhole, starting with the one that will show the least. When using an unpicker for this, place a pin at each end to prevent cutting too far. When cutting buttonholes with scissors, push a pin in at one end and out at the other, snip into the fold of fabric, remove the pin and snip into the holes left by the pin. When working on thick coatings use a punch to make a hole (for the button shank) and then snip to the other end.

5. Begin at the end furthest from the centre front (with vertical buttonholes begin at the bottom) by putting the knot a little way away from the buttonhole on the wrong side, and work a small backstitch. Hold the work as shown and work buttonhole stitch over the edge. Wind the thread around the needle and pull the needle through, then give an extra tug on the thread to settle the knot into its position.

6. Stitches should be as short as possible; this depends on the nature of the fabric, and a slight space should be left between the uprights to allow the knots to lie close together. An uneven edge is the result of working the stitches too closely and not allowing enough room for the knots.

7. At the button end work an odd number of buttonhole stitches, making very short uprights and settling the knots on the surface of the work. This makes a well for the button shank and avoids overcrowding the knots. An oversewing stitch around this end is not as neat and the thread wears through quickly.

8. Work the button end, then work the other end as follows: begin by drawing together the last stitch worked with the first one made at the start of the buttonhole, then work several stitches through the fabric across the end. Pull these fairly tight and make them shorter than the width of the buttonhole; fasten off on the wrong side. On thick fabrics this bar may be loopstitched,

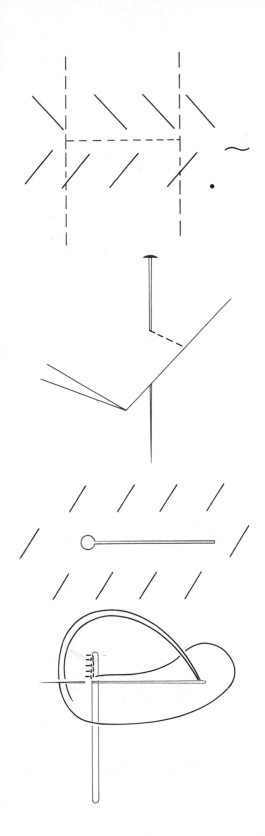

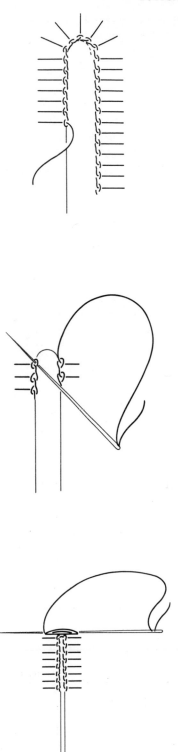

but there is little strain at this point and the plain bar is much less conspicuous.

Method of making Bound Buttonholes

NOTE: These are made through the fabric and interfacing only, leaving the facing free.

1. Cut the patches on the straight grain, making sure they are big enough. Mark the centre of each by creasing along its length with the iron.

2. Place each patch in position with its right side down on to the right side of the work, matching the crease to the marked buttonhole. Baste all patches in position.

3. Turn the work over and machine rectangles. Use a small stitch to prevent fraying. Beginning near the middle of one side, machine around the buttonhole, overlapping the machine stitches on completion to avoid having to fasten off ends of thread. Count the number of stitches worked on the first one and work the same number on all the other buttonholes. The width between the rows depends on the fabric, but it varies between about two or three stitches for fine fabrics and four or five for thicker fabrics.

4. Cut the buttonhole as shown, leaving long points at the ends. Then, using the toe of the

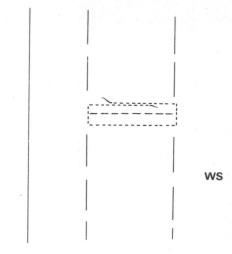

iron, press the join between the patch and the garment.

5. Push the patch through the slit and manipulate the fabric into position so that the gap is filled by two folds of equal width. Oversew these folds together to hold them in position, and press.

6. Turn work to the wrong side and fasten down the small inverted pleats made by the patch. To finish the buttonhole either lift the patch to secure the ends of the buttonhole or on springy fabrics work prick stitch in the join. Press; trim away any surplus patch.

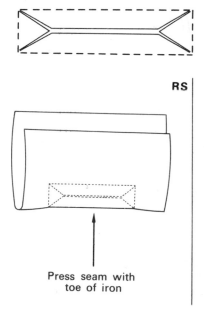

Press seam with toe of iron

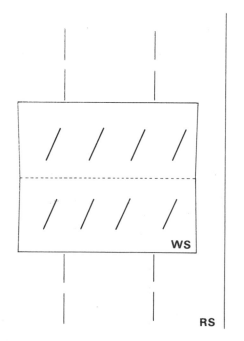

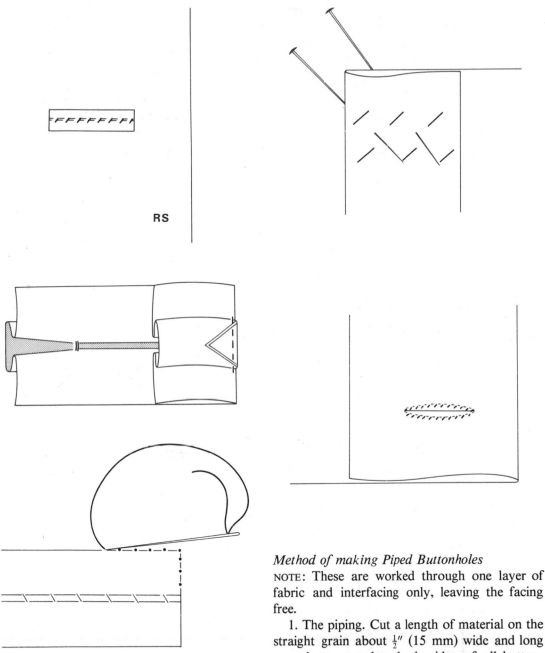

RS

7. After completing the garment, baste the facing in position, marking the exact size of the buttonhole by passing a pin through at each end. Cut between the pins, turn under the raw edge with the point of your needle and quickly hem the edge down.

Method of making Piped Buttonholes
NOTE: These are worked through one layer of fabric and interfacing only, leaving the facing free.

1. The piping. Cut a length of material on the straight grain about $\frac{1}{2}''$ (15 mm) wide and long enough to complete both sides of all buttonholes. Iron Bondina Fusible Fleece to the wrong side; when cool remove the backing paper, and fold the strip in half and press so that it adheres. This piping is now $\frac{1}{4}''$ (8 mm) wide and will need trimming to $\frac{1}{8}''$ (4 mm) or a little more for a thin fabric.

2. Place the piping in position with the cut side on the marked buttonhole. Tack firmly in position and, leaving turnings each end, cut the strip and tack it to the second side. Repeat on all buttonholes. Mark the exact length of the buttonhole with chalk, using the original tacking lines as a guide.

3. Machine the piping in place by stitching with a small machine stitch exactly up the centre of each strip. To avoid having to sew in ends of thread, begin and end at the middle of each strip, also making it stronger with two rows of machining.

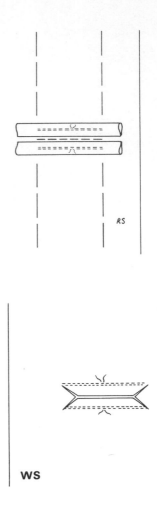

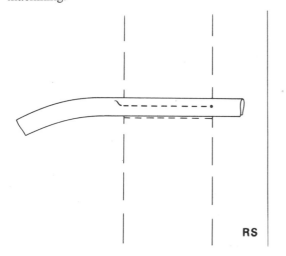

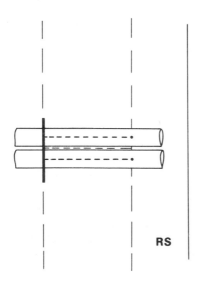

4. Turn the work to the wrong side and cut the buttonholes between the rows of stitching, leaving long points.

5. Push the pipings through the buttonholes—they will immediately lie flat—and oversew the two folded edges with tacking. Press.

6. Finish by working a hand prick stitch across each end as shown, or by stitching across the little triangle of fabric on the wrong side, attaching it to the pipings.

7. On completing the garment finish the facing either as explained in point 7 of 'Bound Buttonholes', or cut a slit in the facing and turn under the edges in a rectangular shape and hem down. The latter method is unsuitable for fraying fabrics.

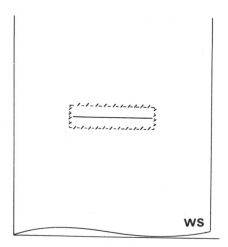

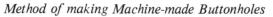

WS

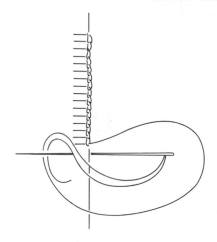

Method of making Machine-made Buttonholes

1. Prepare the work with interfacing and a layer of Bondina Fusible Fleece to hold the fabric together.

2. Mark the buttonholes with chalk, as tackings are difficult to remove later.

3. If the length of the buttonhole can be set automatically, then only mark the starting position with a chalk cross.

4. On lightweight fabrics place a layer of typing paper under the work to prevent it lifting.

5. On most fabrics a better result is obtained by working around the buttonhole twice with 50 thread (Coats' Super Sheen No. 50 or Clark's Anchor Machine Embroidery No. 50).

6. Sometimes a slight loosening of the top tension on the machine produces more attractive results, especially when using the buttonhole attachment.

7. Always work from the right side.

8. Fasten off all ends of thread and cut the buttonholes with care.

BUTTONHOLE STITCH

A strong stitch which forms a knot and is sometimes used purely for decoration. It is often worked over a raw edge to prevent fraying, and in the case of buttonholes the knots take the wear from continuous fastening. The stitches should be as short as the fabric will allow and fairly close together. The knots should touch but not be too close, so therefore it is the thickness of the thread being used which determines how far apart the main support stitches are. Use single thread and wind it around the needle in the direction the stitch is being worked. Tailor's buttonhole stitch is always worked away from the body so that a gimp thread may be held in place with the thumb.

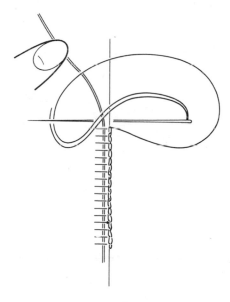

BUTTON THREAD

A strong linen thread used for sewing on buttons, available in a limited range of colours, either in shanks or on reels.

19

C

CASING—for Cord, Elastic, etc.

Cut strips of fabric on the cross about $1\frac{1}{4}''$ (3 cm) wide (or wide enough to take the width of elastic), turn in both edges, tack and press. Apply this by tacking in position and edge-stitching on each edge. Leave a slot for threading the cord by folding the ends of bias strip under before stitching. If the casing is to be used on the edge of a garment, join the bias strip to the right side of the garment and then finish by machining the second side.

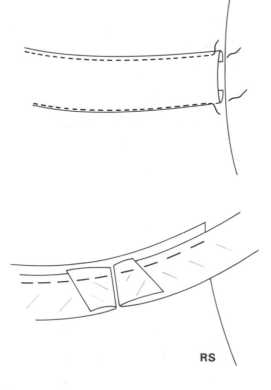

RS

CATCH STITCH

A permanent stitch worked in thread to match the fabric, used for lightly attaching interfacing in position (see also *Herringbone Stitch*). Stitches are normally about $\frac{1}{4}''$ (8 mm) apart and the inner row of stitches falls $\frac{1}{4}''$ (8 mm) inside the interfacing. The thread should not be pulled tight and only a small amount of fabric is picked up on the needle.

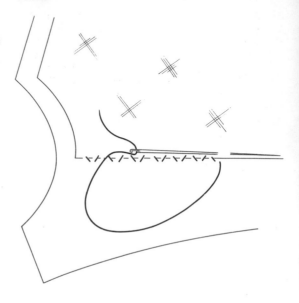

CHALK See *Equipment*

CHECK FABRIC—to handle

1. Study the check to see whether it is unbalanced and therefore to be cut with pattern pieces lying in one direction.

2. With a large check, decide how it can be placed on the garment to look most flattering. The main bar usually looks best if placed below shoulder level horizontally, and kept away from all outside edges.

3. Place the pattern on the fabric to see exactly where the checks will appear. It may be necessary to move a pattern piece so that checks are not distorted.

4. Pleats may have to be re-arranged so that the run of checks is not interrupted.

5. See that there will be sufficient ease in the garment, a tight fit pulls checks out of line.

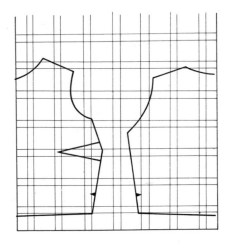

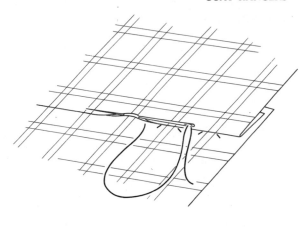

CHIFFON—see *Sheers*—to handle

COAT HANGERS

These should be made in fabric, or in lining on a lined garment, and cut from material on the straight grain. Include a selvedge if possible for added strength. Cut a strip of fabric 3″ (8 cm) long and $\frac{1}{2}″$ (15 mm) wide or a little more. Fold in the raw edge twice so that the selvedge comes on the outside. Keep the edge back a little and hem down. Crease the strip with the iron to mark the centre and pin this to the centre back of the garment. Trim off a little of the loop at each end and turn the raw edge under. Hem this down with deep, strong stitches, working a strong backstitch across the loop $\frac{1}{4}″$ (8 mm) in from the end.

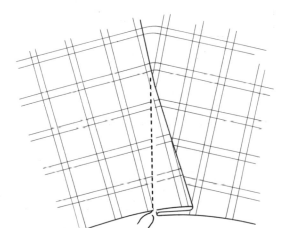

6. The checks should match up at the seams, but where this is made impossible by a dart, then cut out so that the section of seam most visible is matching.

7. It is often easier to slip-tack seams from the right side rather than to try to match accurately from the wrong side.

8. Place pins across the seam picking up the bar of the checks, and machine the seams with pins in position.

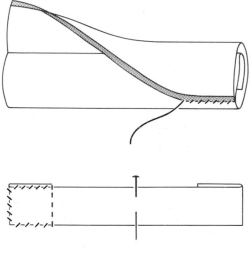

COLLARS

1. *Size*

If any alterations have been made to the garment, then check the size of the collar against the neckline before making up the collar. Furthermore, most collars will set better if they are cut slightly shorter than the pattern (about $\frac{1}{4}''$ (8 mm)). To check this, cut out the under-collar only and pin it to the neckline, using a dress model if available. (If material is short, then a trial collar can be cut in paper, the turnings snipped to enable it to meet the neckline.) Any surplus length in the collar should be pinned out at the shoulder seam.

2. *Cutting*

The position of the grain on the collar is important because it affects the set of the collar when finished. Collars which are shaped at the neckline usually have the straight of grain parallel to the centre back, straight collars should be either exactly on the straight grain or exactly on the cross.

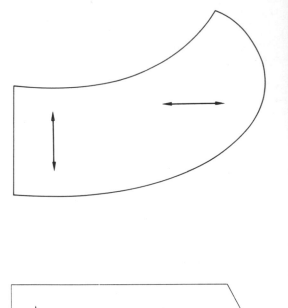

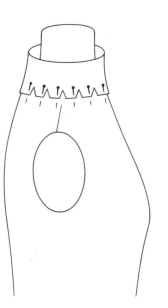

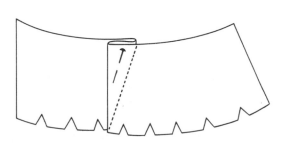

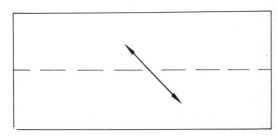

3. *Interfacing*

Interfacings may be taken into the seam (in which case cut out the same size as the collar) and held in place by the machining around the edge, or they may be cut exactly to size (trim away as far as fitting line) and caught to the fitting line. This depends upon the thickness of interfacing being used. Cut the interfacing on the same grain as the collar (the exception being bonded interfacings) and baste it in position on the wrong side of the under-collar. Mark the fitting lines, centre back or centre front, and shoulder lines on the under-collar (this last is usually indicated on the pattern).

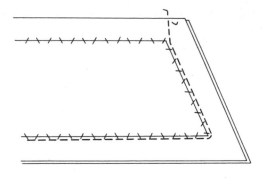

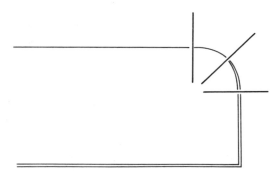

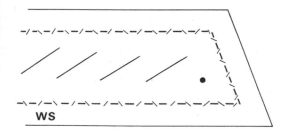

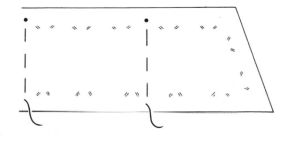

4. *Stitching Collar*

If the collar is to be made up before attaching (see below: 'Methods of attaching Collars'), place the under-collar and top collar right sides together and tack round the outer edge on the fitting line. Machine from the under-collar side. If the interfacing has been cut away, machine just off the edge of it. When stitching a right-angled collar (or any angle less than this), take one stitch across the corner to make it easier to turn through. With curves, mark off the curve itself with chalk lines so that, when machining,

you know that great care has to be taken with this section.

5. *Snipping and Layering*

First press the machine stitching, then trim the interfacing down to $\frac{1}{16}''$ (2 mm), the first turning to $\frac{1}{8}''$ (4 mm) and the second turning to $\frac{1}{4}''$ (8 mm). This lessens the bulk in the edge of the collar and also avoids a ridge because the wider of the turnings will be against the top collar. Next snip all curves in towards the stitching every $\frac{1}{2}''$ (15 mm),

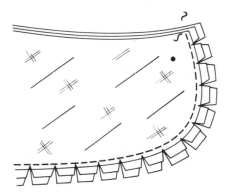

scoop out sharp curves and cut corners well back.

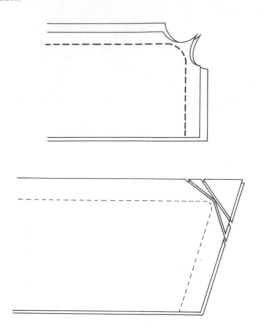

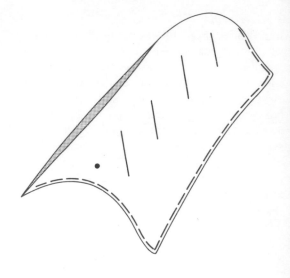

6. *Turning the Collar*

Turn the collar through without the aid of anything pointed, and roll the edges, points and curves until the join is visible. Pull the join very slightly towards the under-collar and tack fairly close to the edge with small stitches. Press the collar. If the style is one that folds over at the neck such as a shirt or roll collar, hold the collar in its rolled position and place a row of basting down the middle to hold the layers of fabric in position.

Main Methods of attaching Collars

The method of attaching a collar depends on the type. A flat or almost flat collar must be attached with facings because the neck-join is liable to show during wear; a stand collar, for example a mandarin style or a roll collar, can be attached without facings (in fact it is better so because excessive bulk is reduced); a shirt collar is often a combination of both methods, the collar being hemmed at the back of the neck where the stand is, but facings are used at the front where the collar is flat.

1. ROLL COLLAR

Interface the underneath half, or stand part, of the collar and, matching the centre back and centre front to the garment, pin the collar right side down to the right side of the neckline. Tack and machine only as far as the fitting line at the

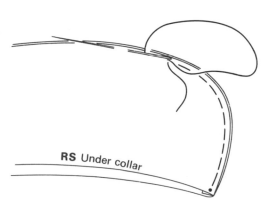

RS Under collar

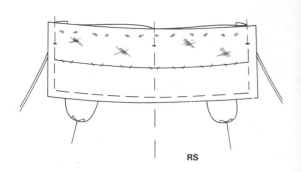

RS

end. NOTE: With this type of collar it is often more convenient to complete the opening, e.g. zip fastener, before attaching the collar. Trim and snip the turnings and press them up towards the collar. Turn in the ends of the collar and tack; turn in the raw edge of the collar and tack. Press. To finish, begin at the centre and bring the collar edge down on to the machine stitches, taking care not to stretch it, pin along the neckline and hem into the machining. Slip-stitch the collar ends.

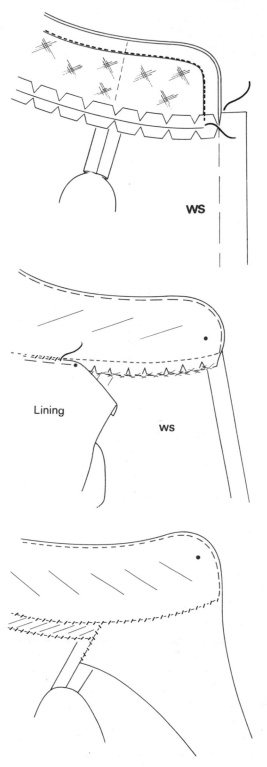

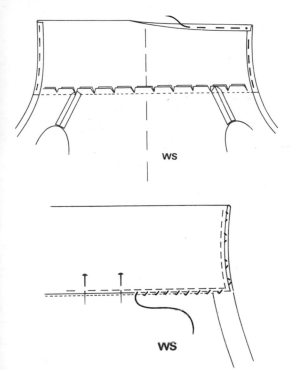

2. STAND COLLAR (Cossack, Chinese, mandarin, ring, etc.)

Attach the outer collar piece to the neckline, snip the turnings and press them open. Tack the inside collar piece to this, right sides together, and stitch carefully around the outer edge on the fitting line. Trim and snip the collar edge, turn, tack and press, and baste the layers together. Finish by prick stitching the join from the right side and then work herringbone stitch over the raw edge. The join is then covered by lining or by a crossway strip of lining hemmed over it. The front (or back) edges are usually finished with a facing. NOTE: If a zip is to be used, put this in before attaching the collar.

In lightweight fabrics these collars can be made up and attached to the neck edge, either using a facing (see method below) or by attaching the edge of the outer collar first, pressing the turnings up into the collar and then finishing as described above for roll collars.

NOTE: If the mandarin collar is in two pieces and there is no opening it must be made up first and attached using facings. Stitch the two collars together at the fitting line before attaching, to prevent having a gap between them.

the corner and then down the front edge. If, for some reason, facings are used across the back neck too, then the whole of the top collar is stitched to the facing. Trim and snip these turnings and press them open where possible with the toe of the iron, to give a good edge. Turn the facing over and tack just below the join, and press. Finish the back of the neck by turning under and hemming into the machining or by bringing lining up over the edge of the collar.

NOTE: For thick fabrics it is easier to attach this type of collar in two parts as explained in Method 1, Roll Collars.

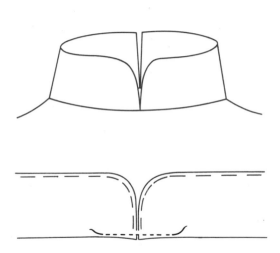

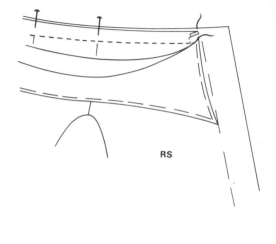

3. SHIRT COLLAR

Make up the collar and pin it to the neckline, matching centre back marks, but pin only the under-collar to the neckline. Tack and machine from end to end of the collar, snip the turnings and either press them open or press them up into the collar at the back of the neck and open only at the front where the facing is to be. Attach the facings by tacking them to the top collar only. There are two rows of stitching to be done now; the first is to attach the facing to the collar and the second is from the end of the collar to

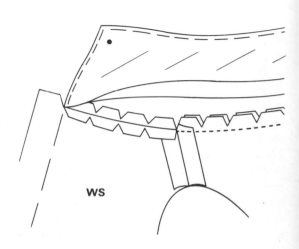

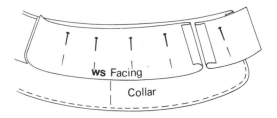

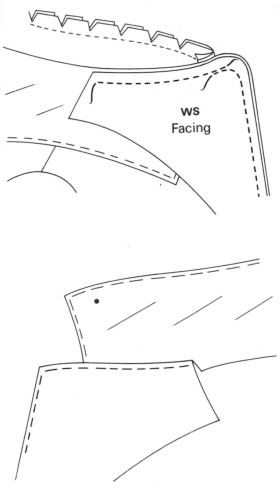

ws Facing

collar upright, smooth down the garment and the facings and tack just below the neck join as shown above for shirt collars. Press in this upright position and then allow the collar to roll.

COTTON

Cotton, the most versatile of the natural fibres, is made from the soft padding inside the seed pod of the cotton plant. Cotton fabrics are soft yet hard-wearing, and they become stronger when wet so are very easy to get clean by hand or machine washing. However, all cotton fabrics are treated with some finish, so washing instructions should be followed if supplied.

Cotton fibres differ in quality and are made into a wide variety of fabrics including organdie, muslin, lawn, lace, plissé, sailcloth, denim, piqué, poplin, cambric, calico, corduroy, velveteen and towelling. Cotton fabrics are cheap and easy to sew, use mercerised or satinised thread and needles of sizes suitable for the weight of fabric.

COURTELLE See *Acrylic Fibres*

4. OTHER COLLARS, USING FACINGS

Make up the collar and, matching up the centre back marks, pin and tack the collar to the neck edge. This may now be machined in position. Remove the tackings and press the machine stitching. Place the facings in position, right sides down, on top of the collar, pin them in position and then make the joins in the facing. Trim these joins to $\frac{1}{8}''$ (4 mm). Working from the garment side, machine slightly below the previous row of stitching to attach the facings. Layer all the turnings and snip around the neck edge. Turn the facings over and, holding the

CUFFS

Cuffs are made of double fabric with a layer of interfacing between. Choose an interfacing suitable for the weight of the fabric. Iron-on Vilene can be used with success as it is a fairly small area that is being covered.

1. Turn-back Cuff

This is sometimes used on straight sleeves, the cuff being cut in one with the sleeve. The seam may be shaped to allow the cuff to lie flat. Mark

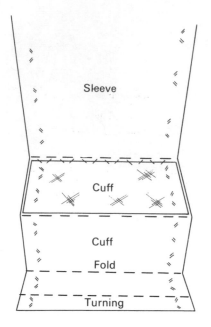

2. Band

This is sometimes used on a long sleeve and may be in a contrasting fabric. Cut out four bands either on the same grain as the sleeve or on the cross for a special effect, and interface the outer bands. Attach the outer bands to the lower edge of the sleeve, snip the turnings and press them open. Join the inner bands to the lower edge, and snip and press the join. Fold the inner band to the inside of the sleeve, tack the lower edge and finish by holding the outer edge flat with herringbone stitch. If the sleeve is to be lined, pull the lining down over the join and hem in position.

all the fold lines and attach interfacing as shown if it is needed. Stitch up the sleeve seam, including the cuff. Press the seam open, snipping the turnings in the cuff section. Turn back the lower edge on the fold line to the wrong side and press it. Finish the raw edge either by working herringbone stitch over it or by turning the edge under and machining it. Fold the cuff back into its position and work a bar tack between the cuff and the sleeve, near the underarm seam.

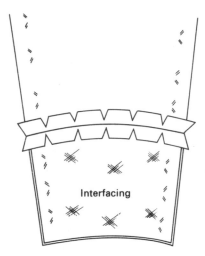

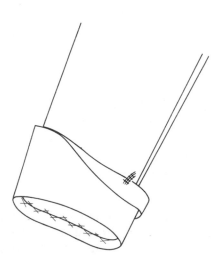

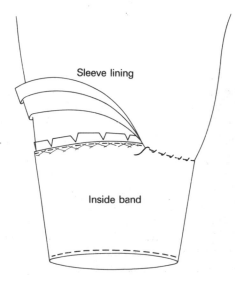

3. *Shirt Cuff*

Straight cuffs are made from one folded piece of fabric, shaped ones are made from two pieces which are joined at the edge. Prepare the sleeve by making the opening, stitching the seam and inserting gathering threads around the lower edge if necessary.

NOTE: This type of cuff may be attached to either side of the sleeve. If working on fabrics such as denim, sailcloth and poplin, or making casual clothes, the cuff may be attached to the wrong side of the sleeve and finished with machining on the right side, but it is more usual to attach it to the right side and finish by hand inside the sleeve.

Interface half the cuff and mark the position of the buttonhole. Place the cuff right side down to the right side of the sleeve and pin the ends. Arrange the gathers and pin and tack in place.

NOTE: A neater sleeve line is achieved if the buttonhole edge is level with the opening, leaving the surplus cuff as an underlap for the button.

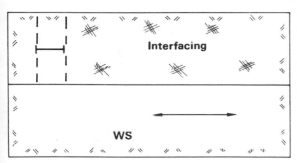

CURVES

Stitch curves carefully after marking them, either using the pattern as a guide or using a cardboard template to ensure that the curve is even. If the fabric frays, use a small machine stitch. Turnings should be trimmed to different widths to reduce bulk and then they should be snipped at intervals of about $\frac{1}{2}''$ (15 mm), closer on tight curves, to allow the turnings to lie flat resulting in a good finished curve. The turnings inside concave curves will open out when the curve is turned through, but turnings inside convex curves

may need scooping out to make sure they will lie flat.

After treating the turnings in this way, turn the work through and roll the edge until the join appears and then tack near the edge before pressing.

CUTTING OUT   See also *Preparation of Fabric*
1. Prepare a large smooth surface. If a table is not available adequate substitutes are a plywood board resting on a bed or a decorator's trestle table. The floor is not comfortable and can lead to inaccuracy.

2. Have ready pins, chalk, ruler and large sharp scissors.

3. Prepare the material and lay it flat.

4. Place the main pattern pieces in position first, checking the straight grain by measuring from the edge of the fabric, and following instructions for placing to fold, etc. Anchor the pieces with one or two pins until the whole layout is complete. Dovetail pieces where possible to economise in material, but watch for one-way effects in checks and florals as well as in the obvious fabrics such as velvet.

5. If any pieces are to be cut twice from the same pattern, for example, a collar, mark round the pattern with pins or chalk and then re-pin the pattern somewhere else.

6. Pattern pieces to be cut on single material should be checked for position and then left on one side to be cut out later.

7. Do not cut out collars or facings at this stage (see *Collars*). Reserve material for them and cut them when needed. There is then no possibility of losing them, and it means that if alterations are made that affect the size of these pieces then they can be cut to size.

8. Having established where each piece is to be placed, return to the beginning of the length of fabric and start pinning. Pin straight edges and folds first. Place the pins diagonally to prevent wrinkling the fabric and put them well inside the edge of the pattern out of the way of the scissors and ensuring an accurate cut edge. Use as few pins as possible. On heavy fabrics either pin through the pattern and the top layer of fabric

only, or dispense with pins, and anchor the pattern with a few objects such as pin box and ruler, and chalk round the pattern. Remove the pattern and cut out on the chalk lines.

9. Cut out confidently with long strokes of the scissors, trying not to lift the fabric and by moving around the table rather than moving the work.

D

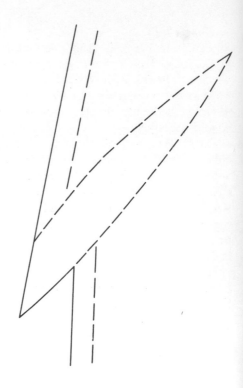

DARTS

A dart is a fold of fabric stitched to a point. The sides may be straight or shaped and the dart can, in some positions, be pointed at each end. In all cases they should be accurately marked on the fabric, making sure the point of the dart is clearly indicated.

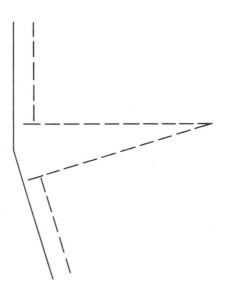

Fold the fabric so that the two sides lie on top of each other, and place pins across the dart so that the material lies flat. Tack the dart, starting at the wide end, and leave an end of thread to indicate the point. Remove tailor tacks and check the length by measuring along the fold of the material, then measure the corresponding dart on the other side of the garment. If the sides of the dart are straight, draw a chalk line on which to machine and mark the point with a chalk line. Press the fold so that the fabric lies flat and machine the dart. Begin at the wide end and place

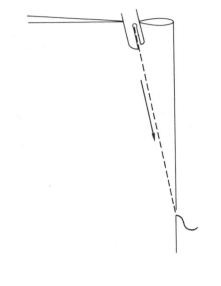

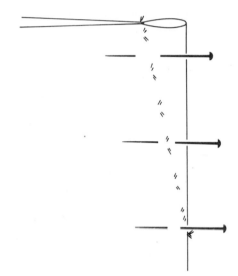

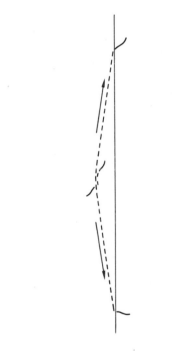

the work under the machine so that the foot is pointing towards the other end of the dart. Double-pointed darts should be sewn in two sections, beginning at the centre and stitching towards the point (see *Direction of Stitching*). Finish the stitching precisely on the edge of the fold. Either sew in the ends of thread or reverse

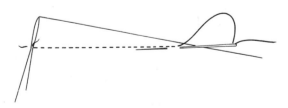

on the machine. If the latter method is used take care to reverse closer to the fold or the line of the dart is spoilt. Press the stitching and then press the dart over to one side so that it lies downwards towards the centre of the garment. With bulky fabrics, split the dart, overcast the edges and press the dart open and the point flat. For more details of pressing darts, see *Pressing Seams* and *Darts*.

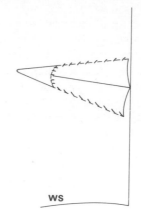

DART TUCKS

These are folds of material similar to darts, but they are left as pleats. Handle as for darts. They may be pressed to one side or pressed with an even amount each side.

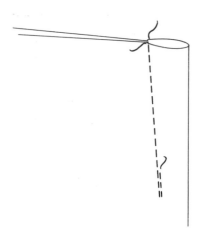

DIOR PLEAT

Often used in skirts, this is an imitation inverted pleat made by leaving a slit in the seam and placing a piece of fabric behind it.

Cut out, leaving wider turnings than allowed on the pattern. Stitch the seam, leaving the length of slit required allowing for the hem. Close the remainder of the seam with small tacks or with a large machine stitch. Press this seam open and complete the skirt. Turn up and finish the hem and then fold back the wide turnings of the pleat and slip-stitch in position. Cut a piece of

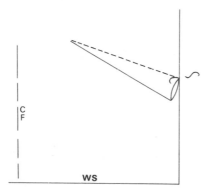

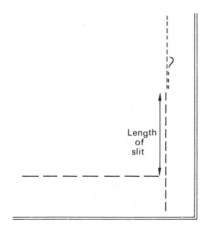

Length
of
slit

material on the straight grain to back the slit, allowing turnings and a small hem and making it *at least 2″ (5 cm) longer than the slit in the skirt*. Turn in the edges so that it is the same width as the turnings on the skirt, and turn up the hem. Herringbone all edges. Cut a piece of lining on the straight grain and place it on the back, hemming it as shown and leaving raw edges at the top. Press and place it right side down on the back of the slit matching the hemlines. Attach by backstitching to the turnings and then work herringbone stitch over the raw edge.

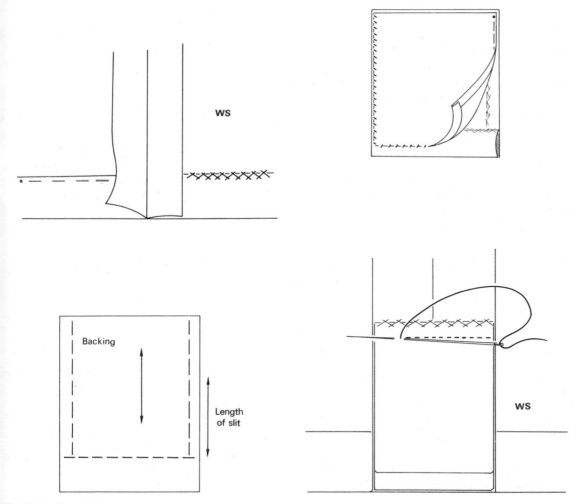

WS

Backing

Length
of slit

WS

DIRECTION OF STITCHING

The final appearance and hang of a garment is greatly improved by stitching seams, etc., in the correct direction, particularly with woollens and loosely woven fabrics. Stitch seams *with* the grain of the fabric rather than against it and also *with* the line of the style, to give a more flattering look. For example, stitch shoulder seams from neck to armhole to avoid a pinched appearance, and stitch skirt seams from hem to waist to avoid a droopy appearance and to keep the grain of the fabric level. In addition, with skirt and dress seams in particular, it is easy to produce a fluted hemline by stitching downwards. Exceptions to this occur when dealing with pile fabrics. See *Velvet* and *Pile Fabrics*.

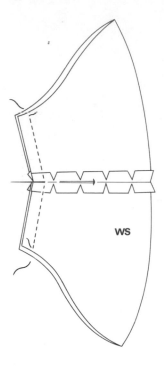

DOUBLE SLEEVES

Short sleeves, made double to eliminate the hemline, look neat and, in washable garments, are much easier to iron. They may be made from two layers of fabric or the inside sleeve may be cut in a lining of a good match.

Cut out two pairs of sleeves and place each sleeve and its lining with right sides together, checking that two right and two left sleeves are being put together. Tack and machine along the lower edge. Snip the turnings and press the join open. Fold the sleeve to join the underarm seam, placing a pin across the join between the lining and the fabric. Machine the seam with the pin in position. Snip the seam a few times and press open. Fold the lining sleeve over the outer sleeve and tack the lower edge, rolling the join slightly to the inside. Press. Baste the two sleeve heads together and set the sleeve into the armhole in the usual way.

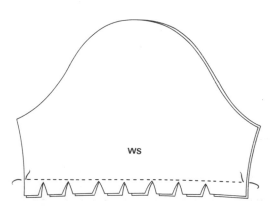

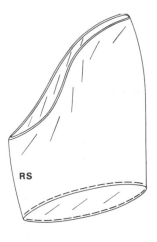

E

ELASTIC—to join
Overlap freshly cut ends of elastic $\frac{1}{4}''$ (8 mm), oversew the edges and loopstitch over the raw edges.

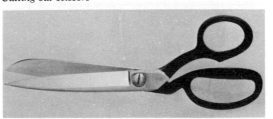

EDGE-STITCHING See also *Top Stitching*
Edge-stitching may be a decorative feature or it may be used to neaten the turnings of open seams (see *Open Seams*). It is worked on a folded edge very close to the fold. Prepare the fabric by turning under the edge and tacking it, keeping the tackings away from the fold. Press and place under the machine with the right side uppermost, that is, with the surplus fabric underneath against the bed of the machine. If worked from the other side the edge of the fabric springs up. Stitch close to the fold, watching the needle, not the machine foot, to obtain an accurate line. Remove the tackings, trim away the raw edge underneath and press.

EQUIPMENT
Most women have at least the beginnings of a collection of dressmaking equipment. The tools should be of the best quality and care should be taken to look after them. Some items are essential before starting to sew, but all should be obtained as soon as possible.

1. SCISSORS. It is worth investing in the best-quality scissors, not only do they give better service but they are easier to handle.

(*a*) SMALL. Have one small pair of scissors with pointed blades about $2\frac{1}{2}''$ (7 cm) long. These are for snipping threads and turnings, and cutting buttonholes. (Some people prefer to use adjustable buttonhole scissors for this.)

(*b*) MEDIUM. A pair with blades of $4''$–$5''$ (10–15 cm) are useful for trimming seams and general cutting of small pieces of material.

(*c*) LARGE. For cutting out, use the largest pair that can be handled. They should have slender

Cutting-out scissors

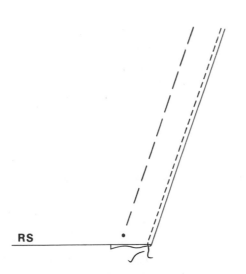

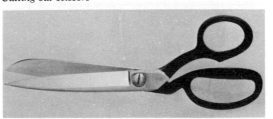

blades from 7″ (18 cm) in length. They are specially balanced and shaped so that the thumb fits into the small hole and the whole of the rest of the hand fits into the larger hole in the handle. The lower blade is flat and rests on the table while cutting.

Care for these scissors by only using them on fabric, never on paper; be sure not to cut over pins, etc.; try not to drop them; keep the blades closed when not in use; never let them become rusty and send them to be professionally ground when they need sharpening.

2. THIMBLE. It is most important that a thimble is not too tight, as the finger swells when it has been enclosed for a short time. The most comfortable type to wear is a tailor's thimble, which is made of steel and is open-ended. This ventilates the skin and so the thimble never feels uncomfortable. While sewing, only the side of the thimble can be placed against the needle and this encourages the correct sewing position (see *Hand Sewing*).

3. TAPE MEASURE. This should be made of fibre glass or linen—other types will stretch. It will last longer if it has brass ends.

4. RULERS. A long ruler measuring 18″, 24″ or 36″ or one metre is useful for chalking seams, etc. Keep a short ruler handy for measuring darts, etc.

5. CHALK. Tailor's chalk is invaluable for marking alterations at fittings as well as for marking material while sewing. White chalk brushes out easily, but the coloured ones are more difficult to remove. A marking chalk made of wax is also available which melts and disappears during pressing. Keep chalk sharp by opening a pair of scissors and shaving it to a sharp edge.

6. STILETTO. This is a long smooth steel-pointed tool with a plastic handle, used for piercing fabric without cutting threads, for eyelet holes, etc.

7. NEEDLE THREADERS. These are useful to those who have difficulty in threading needles and for thick threads.

8. HEM MARKER. This is a particularly accurate method of measuring hems an even distance from the floor. The markers usually have a container filled with powdered chalk, which slides up and down a stand. The marker is set at the required level and chalk is puffed out through a slit in the container. Another type of marker can be fixed to a door and used in a similar way. On pale colours or slippery fabric it is best to use the hem marker as a guide only and insert pins into the fabric.

9. UNPICKER. Used with caution this can be useful for unpicking stitching and for cutting buttonholes, but it is advisable to place a pin in position to prevent the unpicker from slipping and cutting too far.

10. BEESWAX. A cake of wax, sometimes in a plastic holder, used for waxing thread for sewing on buttons. It binds two threads together and coats them with a layer of wax which prevents undue wear on the thread.

11. PENCILS. Keep lead and coloured pencils with sewing equipment for noting measurements, altering patterns, etc.

12. PINS. Use good steel pins bought in a box or tin from a haberdashery counter. They are kept in black paper to prevent rusting. The usual length is $\frac{3}{4}$″ (20 mm), but there are also fine $\frac{1}{2}$″ (15 mm) pins called Lillikins for use on lightweight fabrics, and there are longer pins for heavy fabrics. Pins with large coloured heads are useful on lacy or open-weave fabrics where small ones are easily lost.

13. NEEDLES. Sizes of hand-sewing needles most commonly used are between 5 and 9, but the sizes available are from 1 to 12. They can be bought in packets of assorted sizes or in packets containing all one size, the latter being most useful to the person who sews constantly. The type of sewing needle used is largely a matter of choice, the Sharps needle is a long variety with an oval eye. Betweens or Egg-eyed Betweens are short tailor's needles with egg-shaped eyes. Betweens are used by professional sewers as they are more comfortable to hold and much quicker to use (see *Hand Sewing*).

14. CLOTHES BRUSH. Use for brushing off chalk marks and for brushing up fabrics after pressing.

15. PIN CUSHION. This is not essential and

many people work happily without one. One that slips over the wrist is quite useful when fitting.

16. DRESS FORM. There are many kinds of fixed and adjustable dress forms available and prices vary considerably. A dress form of the correct size is useful, in the absence of a sewing friend, for obtaining a good fit in the main part of a garment, but it does not eliminate the necessity for trying on the garment. A dress form of any kind, however, is very useful for checking the set and size of a collar, for observing the hang and balance of a garment, and for checking major style alterations. A solid dress form is essential also to those people who do their own designing.

17. HABERDASHERY. Items such as fastenings, etc., are bought as required, but a wide selection of oddments is always useful.

18. SOAP. Tailor's soap or laundry soap, used dry, may be rubbed on the wrong side of pleats, seam turnings, etc. When pressed the soap softens and the fabric remains in position longer.

19. THREADS. See under this heading later in the book.

20. PRESSING EQUIPMENT. See under this heading later in the book.

EYELET HOLES

Small holes can be made in most even-weave fabrics by using a stiletto. Push the point gently into the material to move aside the threads and make a round hole which can be quickly oversewn. Make the stitches fairly short. A more decorative effect can be achieved by using a thicker thread such as Anchor Soft Embroidery, and by working deeper stitches.

If a larger hole is required the material must be cut. First mark a circle slightly larger than the hole wanted and then cut it away in quarters, stitching each quarter as it is cut. Use short, even, oversewing stitches or for a raised edge use buttonhole stitch.

F

FACINGS

A facing is a piece of material used to finish an edge. If the edge is straight the facing can be a piece of fabric cut on the cross. If the edge is shaped then one edge of the facing is cut to this shape and it is cut with the grain the same as on the garment itself.

1. *Cutting Facings*

A pattern for facings is provided in bought patterns, but if the style has been adapted or if any alterations have been made it may be advisable to cut new facings. These may be cut directly in material or in paper first, using the garment or the pattern as a guide. The neckline is the most usual place where it is necessary and this is used as an illustration, but the same method of cutting (and attaching) is followed for armholes and waist of skirts or slacks where a waistband is not wanted.

Fold some spare material on the straight grain.

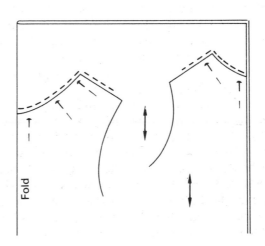

Place the neckline of the pattern on the material and pin on the correct grain, placing to a fold if necessary. If cutting the facing from the garment, fold it at the centre back and centre front and lay the neckline on to the fabric. Mark round the neckline with pins or chalk, and along the shoulder. Remove the pattern. Mark in depth of facing 2″–3″ (5–8 cm) and add a seam allowance to the shoulder. Cut out.

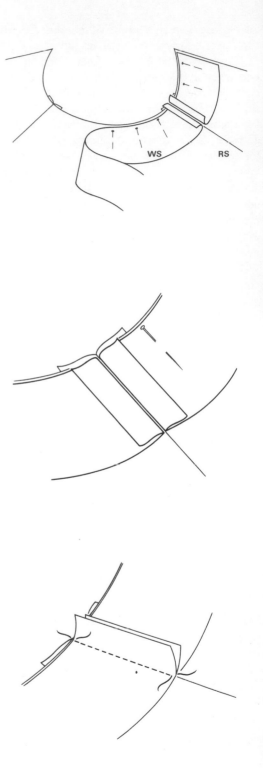

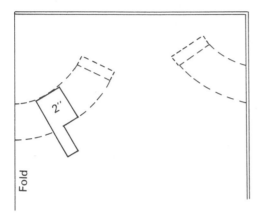

2. *Attaching Facings*

Interface the neckline (see *Interfacing*). Matching the centre front and centre back lines, pin the facings right side down on to the right side of the garment, leaving them free where the joins are to be made. Use a dress model if available. Place work on the sleeve board and press back the ends of facing, creasing them so that they meet in line with the shoulder seam. Lift the facings clear of the garment and match the creases. Machine, trim the raw edges and tack the facings to the neckline. Machine around neck.

Trim and snip the turnings and, using the toe of the iron, run it along the join on the right side of the work. (Omit this right-side pressing on woollens unless a steam iron can be used.) Fold the facings over to the wrong side of the work and, rolling the edge so that the join falls slightly to the inside of the garment, tack a little below the edge. It will remain in position if the stitches are taken through the turnings. Press.

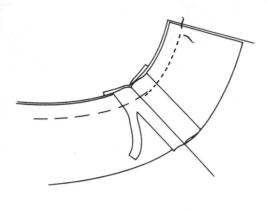

3. *Finishing the Facing Edges*

If there is a lining then the facing can be caught down all round either with herringbone stitch, or by neatening the raw edge and then catching it down. If there is no lining then neaten the edge of the facing and hem or herringbone it only at the seams.

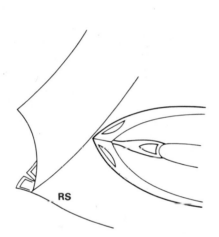

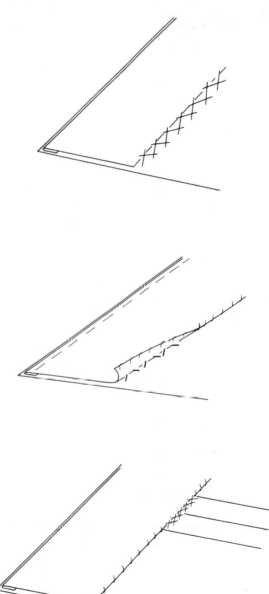

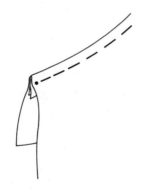

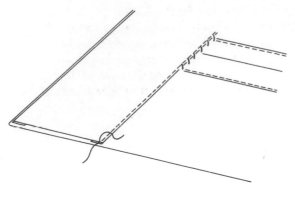

FAGGOTING

Decorative work often forming a lacy effect where pieces of fabric are first hemmed and then joined. The stitch used may be herringbone stitch or a series of ladder-like bars may be worked.

A decorative edge is made by tacking lengths of rouleau (see *Rouleau*) on to tissue paper and then tacking the finished edge of the garment to the paper about $\frac{1}{4}''$ (8 mm) away. Work the faggoting, keeping an even tension on the thread. For thicker fabrics use buttonhole twist. An attractive finish to a woollen dress is a faggot edge of grosgrain or satin.

FAGGOT SEAM

Trim turnings to a little over $\frac{1}{4}''$ (8 mm) and prepare each edge with a narrow hem. Tack and press. Work feather-stitch or some other stitch to hold the hems in place. Tack both edges on to tissue paper and faggot between them.

FASTENERS

1. *Buttons and Buttonholes*—see under 'B'

2. *Frog Fastening*—see page 48

3. *Hooks and Eyes*

The sizes most often used are between size 2 or 3 (for skirt waists) and 00 or 000 for necklines and for lightweight fabrics. Use in positions to take strain. Hooks and eyes are sewn well back from the edge of the garment so that they will not show. If the eye is likely to be visible it may be covered with close loopstitch after sewing it in position. Hooks with straight bars are more useful as they provide a firmer fastening. The bar may be sewn on the right side of the garment and covered with loopstitch to make it less conspicuous. Alternatively a worked bar may be used (see *Bar Tack* for method of making, but loopstitch would not be taken through the fabric).

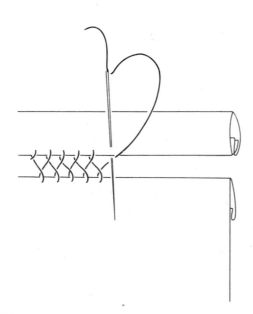

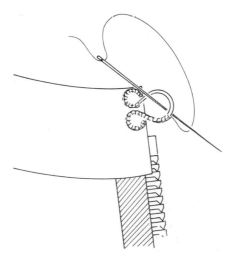

ATTACHING HOOKS AND EYES
Sew on to double fabric plus an interfacing. If there is no interfacing place a strip of tape or skirt binding where the hooks will come. Pin up

the opening, fasten up the hook and eye, and place in position, holding them down with pins. Undo the hook and eye and sew down the head of the hook with several firm deep stitches, then sew round the base with close buttonhole stitch. Sew the eye or bar in position with buttonhole stitch.

by passing a pin through the hole in the centre and anchor it by taking one stitch through each hole, then work four or five buttonhole stitches in each hole. Sew the well of the press stud to the under part of the garment. First pin the opening and put a pin through the centre of the knob section then through the well section and finally into the other layer of fabric. Attach in the same way.

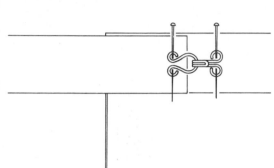

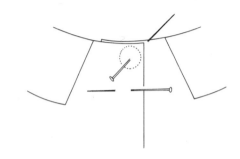

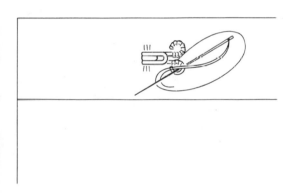

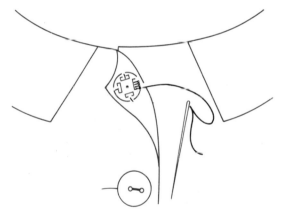

4. *Press Studs*

Useful sizes are from 1 and 2 for heavy fabrics down to 000 and 0000 for lightweight materials. They can be used on openings but will not stand much strain. On loose-fitting clothes they are sometimes used in place of buttons and button-holes with the buttons sewn on top. Often used to fasten the top corner of a front opening.

ATTACHING PRESS STUDS

Sew to double fabric plus interfacing. Attach the dome part, which is slightly flatter, to the other part of the garment. Locate the position

5. *Velcro*

Nylon 'touch and close' strip fastener, made in a variety of colours. The strip is $\frac{7}{8}''$ (2·25 cm) wide but can be cut to required shape as it does not fray. Attach by hemming strongly around the edge or by machining: a small zig-zag machine stitch looks neatest. It has numerous uses, including waistbands, cuffs, collars as well as detachable items such as hoods, bows, ties, jabots, beading.

Enlarged close-up view of 'Velcro'

FEATHER-STITCH

This is a decorative stitch which covers a wide area of fabric, so can be used effectively on hems or overlaid seams, attaching yokes, etc. Work the stitch from the right side, keeping an even tension on the thread so that it looks neat. Make stitches alternately to the left and right. A double feather-stitch is made by working two stitches to each side. Use fine sewing thread or embroidery thread on fine fabrics, on woollens and heavy fabrics use *coton à broder* or Tapisserie wool.

Sew to double fabric, or a separate strip of fabric, so making a fly opening, if there will be a lot of strain.

6. *Zips*— see pages 116–23

FAULTS

A Few Faults and Their Causes

1. Side seams fluting out at hem.	Seam allowance not trimmed away inside hem or seams not stitched in correct direction, i.e. from hem to waist.
2. Puckered seams.	Incorrect thread, stitching done in wrong direction, stitch wrong size for fabric. Fabric not carefully mounted on to lining.
3. Tightness in lined sleeve.	Lining too tight or too short. It should be at least $\frac{1}{4}''$ (8 mm) bigger all over.
4. Puckered neckline.	Stretched during construction. Rectify by tightening with a row of machining.
5. Collar not lying flat.	Neck edge not tacked and pressed with collar upright (see *Collars*).
6. Collar lopsided.	Collar not placed evenly on neck with equal distances between shoulder seam and centre front.
7. Zip appears lumpy.	Fabric stretched on instead of eased or too small a stitch or wrong weight of zip.

FELLING STITCH

Used for stitching lining to coats and jackets and anywhere a fold edge is to be sewn down to a double layer of fabric. Work from right to left, using a very small short needle (Milwards No. 8 Between), taking a fairly deep stitch and bringing the needle up in the edge of the fold.

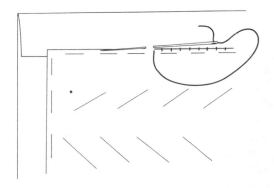

The thread should match the *lining* to ensure that the stitches do not show. There is often slight fullness in a lining which will fall naturally into place between the stitches.

FIGURE PROBLEMS See *Pattern Alterations*

FITTING See also *Bust Dart, Pattern Altera-*
tions

This is one of the most difficult parts of dressmaking. A garment can be well constructed but
still look home-made when worn if it doesn't fit.
A friend who knows as much or more about sewing is invaluable, but if this ideal person is not
available it is worth teaching someone, even a
husband, the basic principles. It is a complex
subject and the only way to really gain knowledge is by experience and often, unfortunately,
by trial and error.

Clothes should be made to fit the individual.
Try them on at every stage of construction even
if you think you already know what needs to be
done, even if you are lucky enough to be of
average measurements. So much depends on the
type and weight of the fabric, whether it is woven
or knitted, the type of lining used, etc. Several
dresses made from one pattern will differ if made
in varying fabrics.

With experience you will discover which patterns and styles fit best with the least amount
of alteration.

Although fitting is so much a matter of making
a particular fabric look attractive and flattering
on an individual, there are a few basic principles
which apply to everyone and to all garments,
and these may serve as a basis on which to build
knowledge gained by experience.

Basic Principles of Fitting

1. COMFORT. An uncomfortable garment will
seldom be worn when it is finished.

2. EASE. Make sure there is ease everywhere;
the amount varies with the position on the body,
but armholes, necklines and sleeves should fit
easily, as well as the bustline, waistline and
hipline.

3. GRAIN. Check the grain of the fabric on
every section of the garment when it is on. With
the exception of pieces cut on the cross the grain
should run at right angles to the floor.

4. CURVES. Style lines can be angled, but
fitting seams should all be gentle curves.

5. FLOW. Do not overfit, let the garment flow
over the figure without catching or wrinkling
anywhere.

6. HANG. Hang the garment from the top,
either waist or shoulders. Begin checking the fit
and smoothing the fabric from that point.

The First Fitting

Put on the garment and fasten the opening with
pins placed horizontally. Sit, walk and raise the
arms to see if there is any obvious constriction.
Stand back and *observe*. Do nothing yet but
look at the general appearance, noting any out-
standing faults, noting any good features which
must remain undisturbed, and observing the
hang and grain line of each section. Look to see
if the hipline and waistline are parallel to the
floor and check that the marked centre front
and centre back lines are centrally placed and
straight. The shoulder seams should lie along the
top of the shoulder and should not be visible
from the front. See if the waistline, if any, is at
the natural waist or, if it is an Empire line or
low-waisted style, that it is in an attractive position for the individual.

Note any of the above points that require
attention and proceed to fit as follows:

Begin at the centre back neck. Check the
centre back line (it may be a seam), check the
grain across the back between the armholes,
check the shoulder dart if any. This dart may

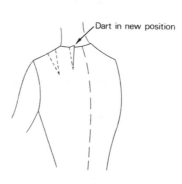

Dart in new position

need moving or making smaller or it may, on an erect figure, be best removed altogether, but if in doubt as to what to do then experiment with it. Any slackness or wrinkling across the back is corrected by undoing the shoulder seams and either lifting or releasing them *on the back only* for the moment. Now move down to the lower

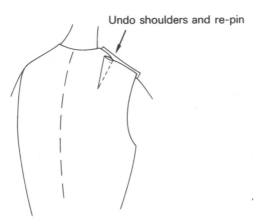

Undo shoulders and re-pin

half of the back and check the centre back line, the waist dart if any, and the side seam (the latter is only a tentative adjustment as these will not be stitched until after the second fitting), smoothing the fabric and undoing and repinning where necessary. The garment should hang from the shoulder and any wrinkling below the armholes may be corrected by lifting the back. Pin out a small tuck across the back to see if this corrects it. If it does, then unpick the back and re-cut the top part, including neck, shoulders and armhole.

Next move to the front of the bodice, check the centre front, the grain across the chest, the neckline, the shoulder and armhole. Check the bust dart, the waist and the side seam. Move on to the back skirt and correct darts, hipline grain and side seams, proceeding in the same way as described above, smoothing and pinning until satisfied. A one-piece dress may be simpler to fit, as alterations to the bodice frequently correct the skirt.

44

Slip one sleeve on to the arm and pin it at the sleeve head so that the grain hangs straight and the sleeve itself is pitched slightly to the front in the natural arm position. Make a couple of check marks across the sleeve and armhole, and when sleeves are tacked in for the next fitting use these as a guide. Mark a tentative sleeve length.

The Second Fitting
First check that alterations made at the first fitting have worked out, then proceed to check and re-fit if necessary the main fitting seams, i.e. side seams. Fit collar and sleeves and finalise the sleeve length. Make sure that openings are all right to complete.

Final Fitting
Check anything which was attended to at the previous fitting and mark the hemline.

If any major alterations or experiments have been undertaken, then of course more fittings will be required.

Method of making and marking Alterations
1. Cut tackings and re-pin in position.
2. If seams are altered, make a couple of chalk marks across the seam as new balance marks.

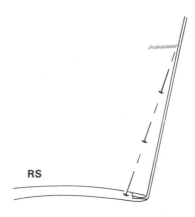

RS

3. Take off garment. Where pins have been used through double fabric, replace with pins on both sides through single fabric.

4. Undo tacking on all seams and spread work out, folded at the centre back and centre front; mark new fitting lines with chalk or tailor tacks.

A Few Fitting Problems and Their Solution

Problem	Solution
1. Gaping neckline.	Undo shoulder, draw up until smooth, re-pin.

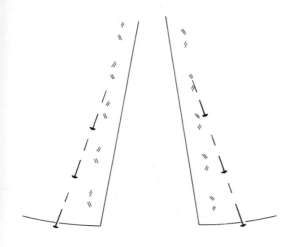

Problem	Solution
2. Stands away at shoulder and arm-hole.	Undo shoulder, release until smooth, re-pin.
3. Back too long, shown by wrinkles across back or grain sagging.	Pin out a tuck across back between armholes to lift back. Undo and re-cut around neck, shoulder, and armholes of pattern.
4. Too wide and loose all over.	Undo and re-cut with a small pleat down centre of each pattern piece.
5. Darts not pointing at prominence or not long enough.	Mark new point with pin. Undo darts and re-mark in new position.
6. Droopy raglan.	Undo and re-pin at a flattering level, taking up surplus.
7. Droopy kimono.	Raise the shoulder and sleeve seam.
8. Wrinkles above bust or up to neck caused by prominent bust.	Enlarge dart width at base (see *Bust Dart*).

5. Mark new balance marks by making tailor tacks through the chalk.

6. Remove old tailor tacks.

7. Tack up and re-fit before stitching.

9. Fabric wrinkles or droops below underarm bust dart.

Re-pin dart to take up surplus; this often gives the dart curved sides.

10. Pulling across bust.

Release side seams; if not enough, make dart wider at base.

11. Waistline on dress drawn up at back or front.

Release shoulder seams and drop.

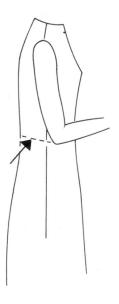

12. Dress catches below bottom.

Lift shoulders, neck may need re-cutting.

13. Dress or skirt side seams slope towards back or front.

Lift front or back shoulder or waist until seam hangs straight.

14. Skirt pulls in below bottom.

Let out seams all the way down.

15. Skirt wrinkles below waist at back.

Undo, hollow out waist at back, running new line from side seam.

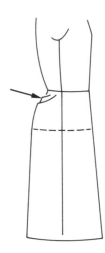

16. Trousers or culottes too low in crutch.

Take pleat across pattern below waist on trousers, and above waist on culottes. Re-pin pattern to fabric and re-cut the top edges.

17. Trousers or culottes too tight in crutch.

Try releasing side seams if hips are also tight fitting, otherwise re-cut the crutch curve slightly lower.

18. Sleeve wrinkles across head.

Release tacks over top of sleeve and let sleeve drop, re-pin.

19. Sleeve pulling across arm at underarm level, or underarm feels too tight.

Undo, cut armhole slightly lower on bodice and on sleeve.

20. Twisted sleeve.

Undo tacks, re-pin with sleeve hanging straight.

FLAP POCKET   See *Pockets*

FOAM BACKS—to handle
Many fabrics can now be laminated on to a thin layer of foam, including jersey and lurex fabrics. As they are fairly thick and springy they need careful handling.

1. Cut out pattern pieces singly (reversing each pattern) on the right side of the fabric.

2. Use sticky tape to attach the pattern in one or two places, as pins make marks.

3. Fit the pattern beforehand; choose simple styles.

4. Use a big machine stitch and release the pressure on the foot slightly.

5. Use a medium-sized machine needle and Coats' Drima thread.

6. Tape the seams.

7. Use iron-on Vilene for interfacings.

8. Make loose linings, never use the mounting method.

9. Press on the right side with a dry or damp cloth, depending on the fabric.

10. When machining, the foam will stick on the machine bed, so either sprinkle with talcum powder or place tissue paper underneath.

FRENCH TACK   See *Bar Tack*

FRENCH SEAM   See also *Seams*
As this is often used on sheer materials it may be desirable to tack it to tissue paper. Tack with the fitting lines together and wrong sides together. Machine $\frac{1}{8}''-\frac{1}{4}''$ (4–8 mm) outside the fitting line. This measurement will be the finished width of the seam and depends upon the thickness and fraying qualities of the fabric. Remove tacks, press the stitching and open the turnings with the toe of the iron. Next trim the raw edges carefully to an even width. Fold fabric over with right sides together and roll the edge of the seam with the fingers until the join appears on the edge. Tack. Press. Machine, using the foot as a guide to keep the seam an even width. If the machine foot slips, through resting on uneven thicknesses of material, place a layer of typing paper underneath.

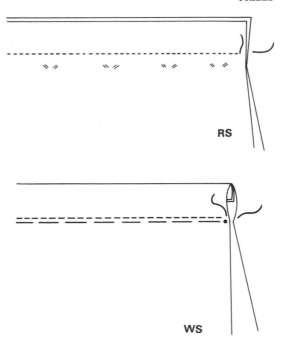

FRILLS
Make frills only from soft fabric that drapes well and gathers easily. Calculate the amount of extra material required by cutting a measured length, gather it up until it looks attractive and re-measure. Now calculate how much is required for the whole frill. If possible cut the frill with the *weft* thread as it will hang better. Double frills are easier to handle if sufficient material is available; cut twice the required depth plus turnings.

Gathering a frill using ruffler

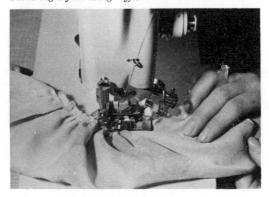

47

Make and press all the joins (joining up both ends if it is to be attached to a sleeve); finish the lower edge. In the case of double frills, fold in half, tack and press. Insert two rows of gathering thread in the top edge and mark the frill off into quarters. Pin at these points with the right side down on to the right side of the garment. Pull up the gathers evenly to fit and pin frequently. Tack, and machine from the gathered side. Finish the raw edges with overcasting or the Mantua-maker's seam—see under 'M'.

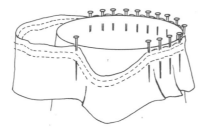

FROG FASTENERS—and Chinese Ball Buttons
A decorative fastening made from cord or from fabric rouleau (see *Rouleau*). Mark out the shape with tacks and stitch cord firmly in place. They may be made on paper first. If using rouleau, keep the seam underneath.

Fasten over a dome button or a button made from cord or rouleau. The thicker the cord the bigger the button.

Frog fastening

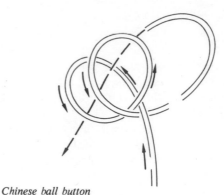

Chinese ball button

FUR FABRICS—to handle
Sewing real fur is a job for the expert, but we can now buy a wide range of simulated fur fabric made from synthetic fibres. These fabrics are by no means inexpensive, so it is as well to handle them with care. Garments made from fur fabrics need plenty of ease. Choose simple styles.

1. Before cutting spread out a sheet to catch the pile. Determine the direction of pile (some curly ones have no particular direction) and note any particular colouring and sheen.

2. Cut pieces singly, using a razor blade or a trimming knife, laying the pattern on to the wrong side and marking round with pins or chalk.

3. Mark turnings on the wrong side with carbon paper and a tracing wheel.

4. Tack seams with tissue paper between the layers of fur.

5. Place a few pins across the seams to prevent slipping and machine *with* the pile with 6–8 stitches to the inch (3–3½ to 1 cm), and using a synthetic thread such as Coats' Drima.

6. Press on the wrong side with a warm iron.

7. On the right side use a pin to pull out any pile that is caught in the seam.

8. Hold down hems with Bondina Fusible Fleece, Jiffytex Adhesive or a large herringbone stitch.

9. Make bound buttonholes backing the area with Bondina Fusible Fleece, using pieces of suede or leather, or a toning fabric, to make the buttonholes.

10. If a zip is needed, use an invisible Alcozip.

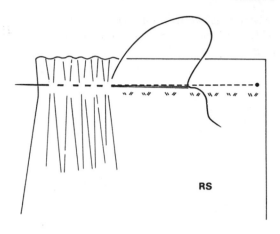

G

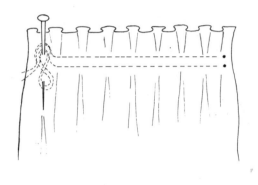

GATHERS

Machine-made gathers produce a more even effect and the gathers are easier to distribute, but the two extra threads can produce a harsh effect on fine fabrics. Set the machine to its largest stitch, loosen the top tension *slightly* and machine just above the fitting line. With some springy fabrics it may be desirable to work another row $\frac{1}{4}''$ (8 mm) above this.

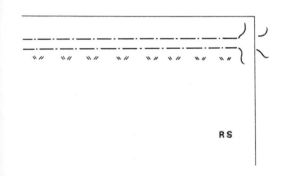

Take hold of the threads which came off the *spool* on the machine and hold firmly with one hand while easing the material along the threads with the other hand.

Hand gathers are made by using single thread and working running stitches along the fitting line. Two rows are usually necessary. Have a knot in the end of the thread and, after pulling up the gathers, wind the ends of thread around a pin to hold.

GRAIN   See also *Selvedge, Warp, Weft* and *Bias*

Grain, also referred to as straight grain or straight of grain, is the straight thread of the fabric as it has been woven. Pattern pieces to be placed on the straight grain should have the pattern marking, usually a long black arrow, placed on a lengthwise thread of the fabric.

GUSSETS

A gusset is a piece of material inserted in a seam to give more room for movement. The gusset has to withstand a certain amount of strain and it is difficult to ensure that the joins are strong.

GUSSETS

Where possible attach by turning under the edges of the gusset section, lay it on to the right side of the garment and machine in position with one or two rows of machining. If it is not desirable to have stitching showing on the right side, mark the exact position of the gusset and mark turning lines on the gusset itself. Place gusset right side down on to the right side of the garment, matching the fitting lines along one side of the gusset. Tack this one side and machine from the *garment* side, reversing the stitching to

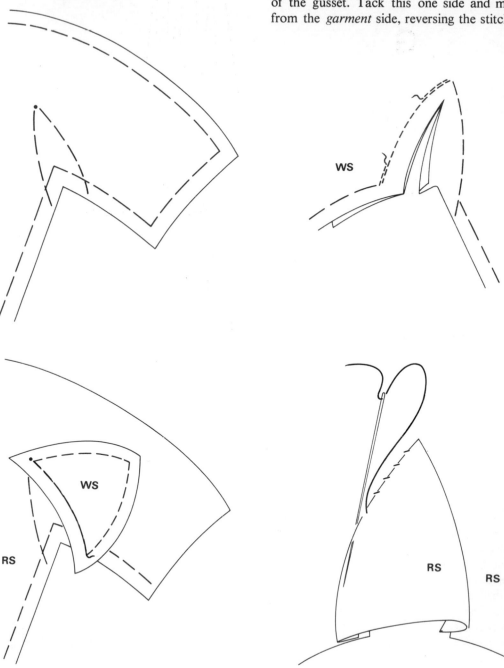

50

finish off. Trim the garment turnings to $\frac{1}{4}''$ (8 mm). Repeat with the other sides of the gusset, leaving one to be sewn by hand. Turn under the edge of this final side, tack in position and slip-stitch. Neaten the turnings on the wrong side.

H

HANDLING FABRICS See under name of fabric

HAND SEWING

Few articles can be well made entirely by machine, and good hand sewing is one of the professional touches that can be applied to garments. When about to tackle hand sewing, be sure there is plenty of time available so that you can acquire an even rhythm and tension on the stitches. Sit comfortably with everything within easy reach. Use short pieces of thread about 12"–14" long (30–35 cm). Long threads tend to knot easily and wear out through passing too frequently through the fabric (tacking threads can be longer). Short threads are used for hand sewing because only the lower part of the arm is moved when a stitch is taken. If a longer thread is used the shoulder, head and back also move and this interrupts the rhythm of the stitches. Take a length of thread from the spool and break it or cut it, thread *this cut end* into the eye of the needle, pass it through and knot it. Knots may be used on most thick fabrics if they are tucked out of sight, but should be avoided on transparent materials or thin synthetics—for these, start with a firm double backstitch.

Perspiring hands should be dusted with talcum powder.

Left-handed people can follow diagrams of hand-stitches by propping the book up in front of a mirror.

HEM MARKER See *Equipment*

HEMS
1. *Marking*
The most accurate way of marking a hemline so that it is parallel with the floor is to use a hem marker (see *Equipment*), but if this is not available, in the case of skirts, an even measurement from the waistline can be taken at intervals. It is not too difficult to turn up a level hem on skirts and dresses which are cut with straight side seams provided the grain of the hemline is observed carefully and the work is kept flat on a table.

The hem level is first marked with chalk from the marker, or pins or tailor's chalk.

2. *Checking*
If in doubt as to whether the length marked will be satisfactory, turn it up and pin it and try it on. Check the actual marking of the hemline by folding the garment at the centre front and centre back so that the side seams are together and the hem is level. Any slight mistakes in the marking can now be seen and corrected with chalk or tacking thread. Next lay the work on the table with the right side outside and with the hem towards you. Work on only a short section at a time when turning up the hem.

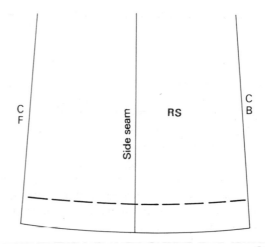

3. *Stiffening, reinforcing or padding the Hemline*

Loosely woven fabrics require some kind of extra firmness in the hemline to improve it, but this can be done to any hem to weight it or to improve the silhouette of the garment.

Fabrics used for this may be chosen from lightweight Vilene, lawn, organdie, tailoring linen, felt, horsehair or polypropylene braid, and even strips of wadding, although this last is more usually enclosed in a bound hem for a padded effect.

Two of the ways in which this extra layer can be inserted are:

(*a*) Cut strips (on the cross if using woven fabrics) and place with one edge on the marked hemline, tack in position and catch both edges lightly to the garment with catch stitch or herringbone stitch. The width of strip should be less than hem depth to avoid having two fabric edges at one point which might cause the hem to show.

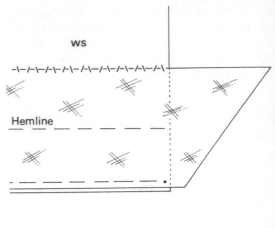

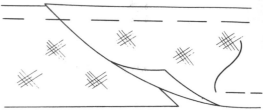

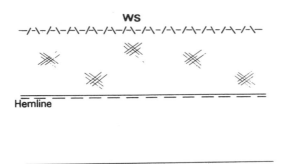

(*b*) Cut wider strips and place in position as shown, catching one edge in place, the other edge will be caught in with the hem edge (either zig-zag stitch or binding—see below).

Join the strips of fabric by overlapping them, but do not stitch a join.

NOTE: Felt is too thick to catch down and would be stitched only where it passed a seam.

Horsehair braid is often applied after the hem has been turned up or, as with lace, stitched to the hemline (see *Lace*).

4. *Turning up a Hem*

Turn up the surplus fabric and tack a little way from the fold. Press this fold on the wrong side of the work in short sections to avoid stretching. Trim down the raw edge to an even width.

5. *Hem Width*

Some articles may have a narrow machined hem about $\frac{1}{4}''$ (8 mm) in depth and this may be used on blouses, shirts, pyjamas, jackets, jeans, aprons, some children's clothes, nightwear, beach wear and some short sleeves. With all other garments the depth varies with the type of fabric and the shape of the hem. In general the more curved the hem the narrower should be the hem depth because of the difficulty of coping with the surplus fabric.

Circular hem on fine fabric (see *Sheer Fabrics*)	$\frac{1}{8}''$ (4 mm)
Flared hem on wool or cotton	$\frac{1}{2}''-\frac{3}{4}''$ ($1\frac{1}{2}$–2 cm)
Shaped skirt ('A' line)	$1\frac{1}{2}''-2''$ (4–5 cm)
Straight skirt	$2''-3''$ (5–8 cm)
Jacket hems and sleeve hems	$\frac{3}{4}''-1''$ (2–$2\frac{1}{2}$ cm)
Overblouses, tunics, etc.	$\frac{1}{2}''-1\frac{1}{2}''$ ($1\frac{1}{4}$–4 cm)

6. *Finishing the Raw Edge*

Choose a method which will be suitable for the fabric.

1. Turn under and machine.

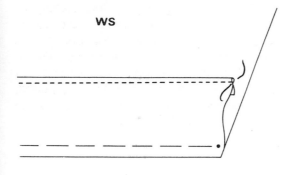

2. Turn under and tack.

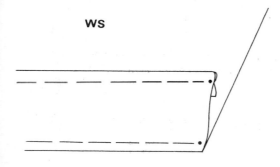

3. Overcast.

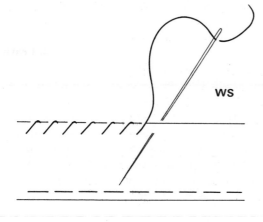

4. Zig-zag by machine.

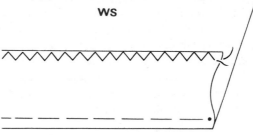

5. Bind.

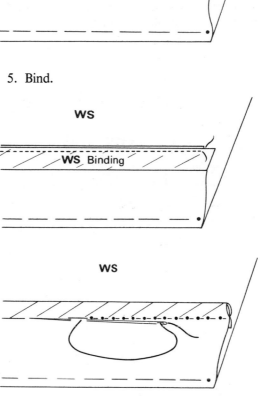

6. Faced hem for weight or to add length. In this most of the hem depth is replaced by strips of lining cut on the cross.

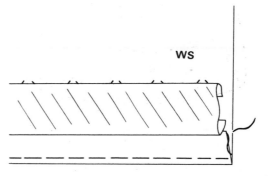

7. *Shaped Hems*

Lay the hem flat and allow the surplus to form flutes. In fine fabrics these may be flattened and hemmed as small darts. In woollens it may be possible to shrink it away, but on very thick fabrics it is best to cut out the surplus material and either overlap the edges and herringbone them or lay the edges together and zig-zag by machine to draw them together.

8. *Stitching the Hem down*

After finishing the raw edge, press the stitching and then tack it flat to the garment. Attach hems that are folded under by slip-hemming, others by lifting the edge and working a loose catch stitch under the edge, picking up only one thread of fabric to avoid pulling threads and so causing the hem to show. Some hems may be sewn down using the blind-hemmer on the machine. Some jersey fabrics are inclined to roll up and these may be caught down by working herringbone stitch over the edge or by working a sloping half-herringbone stitch.

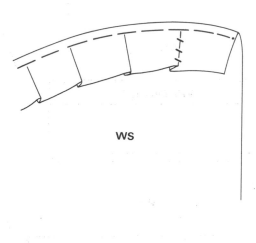

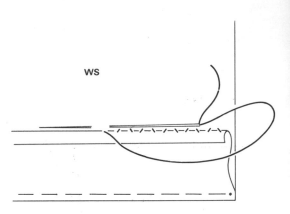

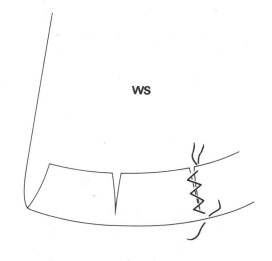

9. *Pressing*

Press in short sections on the wrong side *up to* the hem edge but *not over it*. The right side may be very lightly pressed when the garment is finished and having its final press.

HERRINGBONE STITCH

This stitch may be used for securing hems in thick fabrics or for catching interfacings or hem reinforcements in position (see *Hems*). Work from left to right, holding the work flat and picking up very small amounts of fabric. Leave the stitches loose or they cause a ridge to appear on the right side. The stitch can also be used for joining pieces of interfacing.

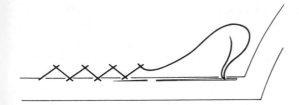

Half-herringbone
This is used where the edge may curl under herringbone stitch. Take the stitch in the garment in the usual way but slip the needle under the raw edge of the hem to make the second part of the stitch.

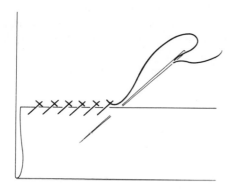

HOOKS AND EYES See *Fasteners*

I

INTERFACING

Interfacing, also referred to as interlining, is an extra layer of a suitable fabric placed in a garment. It may be used to provide strength where there will be strain in wear, for example, buttons and buttonholes, or it may be to add crispness and outline to a style feature on such things as collars, pocket flaps, flat bows. It may be for support, for· example, the front and shoulders of a coat or jacket, or the yoke of a dress. Interfacing is usually placed between two layers of fabric, or a layer of fabric and a layer of lining; it should be attached to the garment, not the facing, and it should be used on fairly small areas.

The choice of type of interfacing is most important, as the appearance of a garment can be ruined by one that is too stiff, but also a limp and disappointing garment can be the result of choosing one that is too light in weight. Choose one that is only *slightly* stiffer than the fabric. Fold the fabric around the interfacing and feel the result before making a decision.

There are both woven and non-woven interfacings available. The non-woven ones do not fray and have no grain, but care should be taken to obtain the correct weight otherwise a rigid appearance can result. Iron-on interfacings are coated with granules of glue which melt under the heat of the iron. These should only be used on very small areas, never where there is any shaping in the fabric, and never on lightweight synthetics such as Tricel nor on softly draping fabrics such as crêpe, nor on any jersey fabrics. Use iron-on interfacings for cuffs, pocket flaps,

55

stand collars (see *Collars*) and in short strips where buttons and buttonholes are to be made.

Choice

Fabric	Vilene	Woven Interfacing
Fine fabrics, lace voile	—	Net, organza
Silk, jersey fabrics	DW2	Lawn (cotton, Tricel, Terylene)
Lightweight synthetics such as Tricel, Dicel, soft brocades	244 Terylene	Organdie, lawn
Lightweight cottons such as poplin, spun rayon, crêpe, velvet, velveteen Lightweight wools— crêpe, bouclé, georgette	A40	Organdie
All medium-weight fabrics, made from wool, rayon, synthetics or blends, corduroy, bouclé, hopsack, heavy brocade, mohair suitings, gabardine	A50 S50 (black)	Soft canvas, wool canvas, holland
Heavyweight fabrics Synthetics and wools Suitings, coatings, flannel, barathea, double-faced cloth, heavy cord, worsteds	255 A65 A80	Collar canvas, flax canvas
Collars, cuffs and small areas; light- and medium-weight fabrics	F2 (iron-on)	Organdie
Heavyweight fabrics	F3 (iron-on)	Canvas, collar canvas

Use of Interfacing

Woven interfacing should be pre-shrunk and cut to the same grain as the section of the garment. Iron-on interfacing should be cut to shape with great care as it will adhere to the ironing surface.

Cut the interfacing, using the pattern or at least using one edge of the pattern as a guide.

Lightweight interfacings (Vilenes: DW2, 1244, A40, organdie, lawn) may be caught in with the seam stitching, so cut them to include turnings. With heavier interfacings turnings will not lie flat if included in the seam so cut them $\frac{1}{16}''$ (2 mm) back from the fitting line to allow the fabric to roll back. Where a piece of garment has been cut in one with the facing (as with coats, jackets, blouse fronts, etc.), cut the interfacing a little beyond the fold line. When the facing folds back it gives a firmer edge and it is easier to get it straight.

Baste the interfacing into position on the wrong side of the work, to the garment, not the facing. Lay the work flat on the table for this unless there is shaping such as a dart. In this case baste around the shaped area, putting the work over your knee to prevent it being flattened.

Attach the raw edges to the garment with catch stitches left fairly loose, or they may in lightweight fabrics be left free especially if held down later by buttons, etc. If the interfacing is stitched in the seam, remember to trim it down before pressing.

INTERSECTING SEAMS

Where two pieces of seamed fabric are to be joined, reduce the bulk of the turnings as much as possible by trimming to $\frac{1}{8}''$ (4 mm) before making the join. After joining make a small snip through the turning to enable it to lie flat.

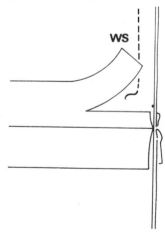

WS

INVERTED PLEAT See *Pleats*

J

JERSEY FABRICS

Most fibres can be knitted into jersey fabrics of various weights and they are popular as they are comfortable to wear. This is mainly because they are soft and, due to their structure, they give with the movement of the body. Fibres used for jersey fabrics include wool, Terylene, (Crimplene), Courtelle, Tricel, Nylon, Acrilan, silk and cotton. Cotton is used mainly for knitted fabrics to be made into underwear, nightwear, sportswear and children's clothes. Jersey fabrics range from plain firm suit-weight fabrics to light lacy knits and they are also made to look like woven fabrics on the right side. These fabrics are not difficult to sew and good results can be obtained if the following points are noted:

1. Choose a style suitable for the type and weight of the fabric. Check the pattern layout as all pieces will have to be cut lengthwise, that is, with the direction of the knitting.

2. Look carefully at the cut end of the fabric as many jerseys are pulled out of line. Cut the end straight, press out the centre fold and pin the edges together.

3. Lay the fabric on the table without stretching, and press out any ripples with a damp muslin. Place the pattern pieces having regard to the rib as well as the pattern. Cut out with very sharp scissors.

4. Good mounting fabrics are jersey nylon or Tricel jersey as the properties of the fabric are then retained, otherwise loose-line with a lining of suitable weight for the jersey.

5. Make open seams; if turnings tend to curl up then loopstitch them by hand.

6. Use a machine needle suitable for the weight of the fabric and either pure silk thread or synthetic thread, such as Coats' Drima, as both these threads will stretch slightly with the fabric. Stitch with about twelve stitches to the inch (five to 1 cm). Use a light zig-zag machine stitch if possible which will prevent seams splitting in wear, otherwise pull the work very slightly as it goes under the machine foot.

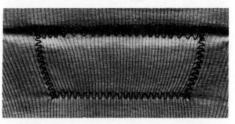
Stretch stitch for jersey fabrics

7. Tape the shoulder seams and either stay-stitch necklines or quickly baste the interfacing or mounting in position to prevent stretching.

8. Avoid top-stitching on plain jerseys as the machining is unlikely to run parallel with the ribs of knitting and may appear uneven.

9. All types of buttonhole are suitable for jersey fabrics. The decision will depend on the weight of the fabric.

10. Facings may need to be caught down with herringbone stitch.

11. Press with a steam iron on the wrong side. (Cover with a slightly damp muslin when pressing on the right side.)

JETTED POCKET   See *Pockets*

K

KNITTED FABRICS   See *Jersey Fabrics*

L

LACE FABRICS

1. Choose simple styles or those which have been specially designed for lace.

2. Examine the design carefully before cutting out. If using lace flouncing, fit the pattern carefully and then cut out so that the scallops form the hemline.

3. Make up on its own to retain the transparent effect, trying to avoid having the lace double at any point. Use net or organza for facings and hems and choose one of the following seams:

(*a*) Machine, trim down and overcast or zig-zag the edges together.

(*b*) If the lace is loosely woven work the same seam as (*a*) but work a second row of machining before overcasting.

(*c*) Invisible join. Cut out with large turnings with special regard for the placement of motifs where the side seams are to be joined. After cutting out and marking turnings, lay the front over the back and match the pattern as far as possible. It will be found that where a seam is shaped it is not possible to match up complete motifs, but with straight seams and a small pattern it is easily done. With a loose-fitting style the seams may be moved slightly to match the pattern. To make the seam work either satin stitch on the right side, by hand; or use a close zig-zag stitch on the machine, first placing tissue paper under the work. In both cases follow the main outline of the pattern and then trim away the surplus lace close to the stitching on both sides.

4. For an opaque effect mount lace on to taffeta and work open seams.

5. Keep turnings well trimmed and avoid top-stitching.

6. Use machine-made buttonholes.

7. A crisp effect can be given to the lace by mounting it on to net, and the hems of long dresses can be stiffened with horse-hair braid or polypropylene braid.

8. Lace can be bonded to a backing by using Bondina Fusible Fleece, but try it out on a small area first as its success depends on the type of lace being used.

9. Edges can be attractively finished with bindings of chiffon or georgette.

10. To press, place lace right side down on to a folded Turkish towel and use a steam iron or a moderately hot iron and a damp cloth.

LACEY OPEN FABRICS

These open fabrics are made from synthetic fibres or from wool (often mixed with mohair) and are either woven in open patterns or knitted. They are soft and light in weight, and garments made from them are inclined to lose their shape, so unless a transparent effect is especially desired it is best to mount the garment on to a suitable lining.

Raw edges ravel easily, so stay-stitch, or neaten the edges of each piece after cutting out. Use a fine machine needle and sew with a fine thread. Tack and baste with machine embroidery thread that will not damage the fabric (e.g. Anchor Machine Embroidery No. 50). Replace the normal machine foot with a short stubby foot that will not catch in the open fabric. (This foot is usually provided for the purpose of working quilting.) Press these fabrics with the right side down on to a Turkish towel.

LAPPED OR OVERLAID SEAM

Fold under the turning of one piece of fabric, tack and press, taking care not to stretch it. Place it in position over the second piece of material, matching up fitting lines, and pin the seam, starting at the centre. Tack and press, and stitch from the right side either by machine or using a decorative hand stitch.

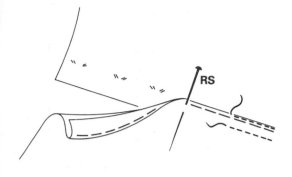

LEATHER AND SUEDE

1. Choose a simple style with few seams. Fit and alter the pattern making sure there is sufficient ease as there is no give in the skins.

2. Chalk around the pattern and cut out singly. Never use pins.

3. To fit, stick the main pieces with sticky tape.

4. Tape all seams and trim away surplus leather afterwards. Turnings can be stuck down with adhesive.

5. Interface with a soft iron-on type (e.g. Iron-on Vilene F3).

6. Use a large machine stitch and a heavy needle. Avoid hand sewing.

7. Edges should be turned under and machined, or add a piping and turn under and machine.

8. Make bound or piped buttonholes and use a heavyweight zip or invisible Alcozip.

9. Do not attempt points in collars, etc., but make rounded corners.

10. Press on the wrong side with a warm iron over brown paper.

11. Either machine stitch hems or turn up and stick with an adhesive such as Jiffytex.

LINEN

Linen fabrics are made from the inner part of the stalk of the flax plant. The materials are very strong and hard-wearing, and are heavier than cottons. They tend to be expensive and so are not used to a great extent for clothes, but linen is still used for a number of household items. It is strong, drapes well and is very absorbent: it creases easily, but dress linens and suitings are treated to make them crease-resistant, or at least given a degree of crease-recovery. Close imitations of linen are made from rayon and also from synthetic fibres (usually Terylene), and these are referred to as 'linen look' fabrics.

LINING

There are two main methods of lining.

1. *Loose-lining*
For this method the garment is partly made up, the lining is also partly made and then the lining is put against the garment, right side up, so covering seams, etc., and it is attached at the edges. Reasons for choosing this method are those of appearance (jackets and coats), comfort (where rough fabrics are used) and warmth. For details see *Loose-lining* below.

2. *Mounting (also called Backing or Under-lining)*
For this method, after cutting out the garment pieces, use the same pattern again and cut out in a suitable fabric (not necessarily lining). Each piece of fabric is placed against its backing fabric, basted in position and thereafter treated as one layer. Mounting a garment will improve its silhouette, give it more body, prevent it losing its shape through seating, lessen its tendency to crease, make it softer against the skin, lengthen its life, make washing garments easier to iron and prevent clothes that are dry-cleaned from going limp. Most fabrics are improved by mounting, and garments will generally perform better in wear provided the correct backing fabric is chosen.

On the whole it is best to choose a mounting fabric that is *lighter* in weight and *also softer* than the outer fabric. A mounting fabric that is too flimsy and soft will result in a droopy garment, and a garment that has been mounted on to a fabric that is too heavy or stiff will lose its characteristics because the lining's properties will tend to be too obvious. Choose a fibre that will react to washing and dry-cleaning in the same way as the outer fabric, and if possible one that comes roughly within the same range of ironing temperatures.

A combination of both methods is possible, depending entirely on the fabric, it may be desirable to both mount and loose-line, and this is often done with jackets, coats and skirts made from open-weave fabrics. On the whole dresses become too bulky if both methods are used.

Fabrics for Loose Linings

Crêpe de Chine (for medium-weight fabrics).

Jap silk (for very lightweight fabrics such as silk).

Silk taffeta (if available, ideal for all light- and medium-weight woollens and blends).

Bemberg silk (not always available, a good-quality rayon taffeta).

Dicel (a soft type of rayon of medium weight).

Taffeta and satin (inexpensive rayon linings, cheapest ones do not wear well).

Tricel (a type of rayon, only for medium and heavy fabrics).

Milium (satin-backed with a coating of aluminium which insulates, for heavy fabrics only).

Fabrics for Mounting

Net (for lace).

Organza, Terylene georgette and crêpe (for sheers).

Chiffon (for embroidered chiffon).

Nylon jersey (for jersey fabrics and harsh fabrics that will not loose their shape).

Lawn (cotton, Tricel, Terylene, depending on the outer fabric, for use with light- and medium-weight fabrics).

Taffeta (rayon, Tricel, Dicel, silk for all medium to heavy fabrics). Jap silk (for lightweight fabrics only).

Silesia or fine calico (close cottons, use with tweeds, woollens, etc.).

NOTE: Some good-quality fabrics such as worsteds, flannels, etc., will not require mounting, and many jersey fabrics and bonded fabrics are best used alone.

LOOPSTITCH

Sometimes called blanket-stitch, which is often a fancy version used on blankets and for embroidery. Loopstitch is used for neatening

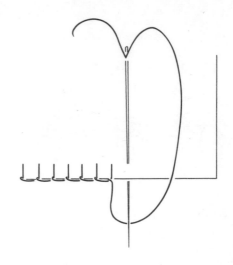

seams on fabrics that do not fray too much, on jersey fabrics to prevent edges from curling up, and it is very useful for working over short sections of raw edge where seams have been clipped, etc. See also *Belt-loops, Fasteners* and *Bar Tack*.

LOOSE-LINING   See also *Mounting*

Method for Jacket or Coat with Collar

1. CUTTING THE LINING

The lining should be slightly looser, so when cutting out allow a little extra on all edges. Cut the back-lining to a fold and allow about 1" (2·5 cm) for a pleat down the centre back for ease (this may be allowed for on the pattern).

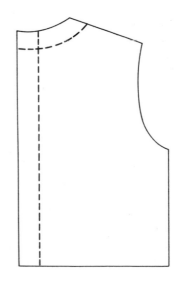

After cutting out, tack this pleat and press it to one side, leaving the tackings in position until the garment is complete. The lining in a jacket should be $\frac{3}{4}''$ (2 cm) shorter than the jacket when finished, plus a good turning allowance. A coat lining when finished will be about 2" (5 cm) shorter, but allow about 2" for the hem on the lining. If the collar is of the stand type or a normal tailored coat collar where the neck-join will not be visible it is unnecessary to use a facing at the back of the neck, in fact it is undesirable because of the additional bulk. When cutting the back-lining for these styles check the pattern and make sure it will come up to the neckline.

2. ATTACHING THE LINING

Fit and make up the jacket including side seams, pockets, etc., and attach the front facings but omit the shoulders and collar. Make up the lining on to the same stage (use open seams; neatened by machining). Remember to machine slightly outside the fitting line to make the lining bigger than the jacket.

Press lining and jacket, lay jacket out on the table wrong side up and lay lining carefully on it with right side uppermost. Match up the centre back, seams and darts and, beginning at the centre back, attach the lining with rows of basting, leaving about 2" (5˙ cm) free around the outer edges. As the lining is bigger it will form slight pockets of fullness. Take care not to smooth the lining entirely flat or stretch it lengthways, or it will cause the garment to pucker when worn. Where darts or shaped seams occur these must be kept together and it helps to lift the work slightly to retain the shape.

Turn under the raw edges of lining on the front facings. Turn up and finish the hem, and turn under the lining and tack it down, being sure to pull it back slightly to avoid stretching. Complete the construction of the shoulders and collar; line and set in the sleeves (see *Sleeves*). Stitch the front shoulder lining to the shoulder seam and bring the back-lining over it, turn under and tack. Tack the lining across the back of the neck. On a coat the hem is now finished (see 'Finishing Hem and Corners' below). Finally, work felling stitch to hold the lining in place.

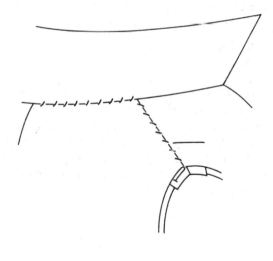

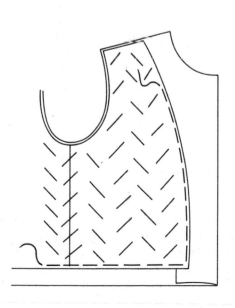

*Method for Collarless Coats or Jacket (Chanel,
    Cardigan, etc.)*

It is slightly easier, especially for a beginner, to
make a collarless coat or jacket, and a different
method of lining it can be followed. Instructions
for cutting the lining are the same as explained
above for 'Method for Jacket or Coat with
Collar' except that the lining for the jacket back
will be cut slightly lower as a fabric facing will
be used at the neck.

Work the shaping and shoulder seams of the
garment and attach the front facings and neck
facings, taking care that the weight of the garment does not stretch the neckline while this is
being done. Make up the lining to the same
stage, press, and lay it in position on the jacket,
matching up seams and shaping. Baste in position (see previous method). Turn under the
edges of lining around the neck and front edges,
and tack. Join the side seams on the outer fabric
only. Turn up the hem at this stage on both
coats and jackets. Finish the lining side seams
by felling the back over on to the front, and
finish the hem by felling it down (for a jacket) or
by making a separate hem (coats).

Finishing Hems and Corners

Turn up the hem with the facing opened out and
finish the hem edge. Trim down surplus fabric
inside facing. Fold facing back into position,
slip-stitch the folded edge and work buttonhole
stitch over the raw edge where it will be visible
below the lining. (This short section may be
bound with a crossway strip of lining if the coat
hem is also bound.) On thin fabrics turn this part
under and hem it down.

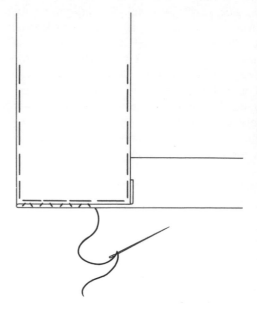

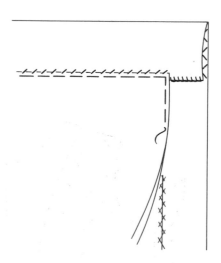

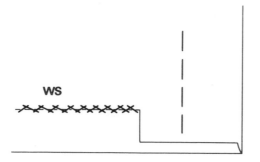

Turn up and finish the hem of the lining with
slip-hemming, and fell it down at the corners.
Attach the lining to the coat hem at intervals
with bar tacks made $\frac{1}{2}''$ (15 mm) long to allow
the lining to move independently.

Lining a Skirt

1. Cut out the lining after fitting the skirt itself so that any alterations may be made straight away in the lining. Use good-quality, strong lining for skirts, and tack it and fit it as carefully as the skirt itself. The lining will not prevent seating unless it fits as closely as the skirt, and a half lining will not be effective unless it comes below the seat.

2. Stitch and press the lining darts and seams, and hang it inside the skirt. Match up the seams and baste the two together around the waist. Baste down each seam to within 3″ or 4″ (8 or 10 cm) of the hemline. Finish the waist (see *Waistband* and *Waistline Finishes*).

Mark, turn up and finish the skirt hem. Turn up a hem on the lining about 1″ (2·5 cm) in depth, making it about 1″ (2·5 cm) shorter than the skirt. Work a bar tack $\frac{1}{2}$″ (15 mm) long at each seam to attach the lining to the skirt.

Pleats

Where a knife pleat occurs, leave a slit in the lining equal to the length of the pleat. If the pleats are grouped it may be best to cut a section out of the lining.

Dress Lining

A loose lining in a dress is usually attached at the neckline (and waist if any). Fit the dress and work the shaping, side seams, shoulder seams and opening. Make any necessary alterations to the pattern and cut out the lining. Stitch darts and side seams. Turn the dress inside out and slip the lining on to it (use a dress model if possible). Match up the centre front lines, darts and seams, and baste the lining in position, making sure it comes right up to the neck and shoulders.

Finish the shoulders of the lining as described earlier under 'Method for Jacket or Coat with Collar'. Attach facings or collar to the neckline in the usual way and finish the armholes.

The lining may be attached down the side seams of the dress with $\frac{1}{2}$″ (15 mm) bar tacks worked at intervals of about 8″ (20 cm).

M

MACHINE FELL OR FLAT FELL SEAM

Tack and machine on the fitting line with either the right or wrong sides of the fabric together, depending upon the effect that is required. The seam, when finished, will show two rows of machining on one side and one on the other side.

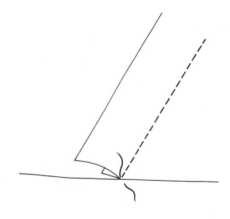

Remove tacks and press the stitching. Open the seam with the toe of the iron and then press both turnings towards the back of the garment. Trim away the underneath turning to $\frac{1}{4}$″ (8 mm)

63

(or the desired width of the finished seam). Trim the upper turning to an even width $\frac{1}{4}''-\frac{1}{2}''$ (8–15 mm), depending on the thickness of the fabric. Turn this edge under and pin and tack, starting at the centre of the seam and working towards each end to avoid stretching. Press this folded edge and then machine close to the fold. Either side may be used as the right side.

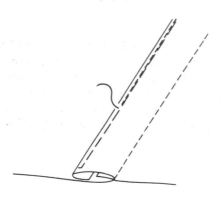

MACHINES

With so many makes available it is not possible to cover their workings in detail. However, some information on general care of sewing machines, and adjustments to be made when faults occur, may be found useful.

Sewing machine

Care of Domestic Sewing Machines

1. If the machine is to be used a great deal it should be oiled and dusted every week, but if it only comes out for occasional use then attention every couple of months will be sufficient. Less often than this, parts should be unscrewed or opened and cleaned and oiled once every year, and it is worth taking the machine to a reputable agent to have it completely overhauled.

2. Oil after use, not before, apply small amounts regularly to moving parts and obvious oil-holes (these are marked on some makes, e.g. Bernina), but take care not to get oil on the belt of an electric or treadle machine or it may begin to slip.

3. It is best to remove the needle before oiling as oil can accumulate in the groove.

4. A drop of oil in the bobbin case will help it to run smoothly.

5. Remove accumulated fluff, polish steel parts with a duster, tighten all screws and run the machine without threading, then replace the needle and run it again on fabric but still without threading. Do not use it immediately, but leave overnight with a piece of material under the foot.

A machine which is habitually kept in a cold possibly damp cupboard or upstairs room will benefit greatly and run more smoothly for being kept in a warm living room for a few weeks now and again.

Using the Machine

1. Replace needles often—say, a new one for every garment made—and use the correct size of needle for the fabric.

2. Use the same thread above and below except for some types of embroidery.

3. Before threading, check that the spool case is quite free of scraps of thread and fluff.

4. When sewing, place the work right under the foot, turn the wheel until the needle is lowered into the fabric, lower the foot, and then turn the wheel once more in order to work the first stitch. This procedure should prevent jamming, but if the machine feels at all stiff or jams then unthread it and remove all possible thread.

Remove the spool, spool case and throat plate, and then search for the scrap of thread which has caused the jamming.

5. Keep a small brush handy to brush out the feed teeth, especially after working on fluffy fabrics.

6. ELECTRIC MACHINES. Check plug, flex, light bulbs, etc., from time to time for wear and loose screws.

Size of Needle—see also *Threads*
For correct size of needle for machining various fabrics, see *Needles*.

A Few Common Faults in Machining
PUCKERING SEAMS
Check: 1. Incorrect thread.
      2. Different thread top and bottom.
      3. Wrong machine foot, where a selection is provided for embroidery, etc.
      4. Tension too tight.

MISSED STITCHES
Check: 1. Needle in wrong way round.
      2. Needle not inserted far enough. .
      3. Blunt needle.
      4. Thread too thick for needle.
      5. Needle threaded wrongly.

STITCHES VARY IN SIZE
Check: 1. Needle in wrong way round.
      2. Stitch-size indicator not screwed up and therefore moving.
      3. Insufficient thickness on sheer fabrics (use tissue under or typing paper).

BREAKING THREAD
Check: 1. Wrong threading of top or bottom thread.
      2. Tension too tight on top thread.
      3. Rough section of thread forming a ball of fluff at needle eye.
      4. Blunt needle.
      5. Fine thread with too thick a needle.
      6. Different thread top and bottom.

Sewing
1. After plugging in and winding spool, release spool-winding mechanism, tighten balance wheel.

Insert spool carefully, taking care the thread goes right into the correct grooves. With machines with a spool case, take care that it is inserted correctly in the socket.

2. Thread top of machine and raise the spool thread. Hold the spool thread loosely in left hand and turn the balance wheel towards you slowly and watch the needle descend. The top thread circles the spool case and picks up the lower thread (in some machines you can watch this by leaving open the spool-case cover). Finally pull the top thread gently and the lower thread will appear through the needle hole in the plate.

3. See that the needle is at its highest point by turning the balance wheel towards you.

4. Take both threads towards the back and between the toes of the machine foot.

5. Place work completely under needle, turn balance wheel towards you until the needle is in the fabric, lower the presser foot and begin machining. Start gently by turning the balance wheel for the first stitch and then take over with the electric motor, handle or treadle.

6. At the end of the row stop machining by slowing down and placing a hand on the balance wheel; one final stitch may need to be made by turning the wheel.

7. Raise the wheel to its highest point by turning the wheel towards you, lift the foot and take the work out to the back using both hands so that the threads may be cut on the thread cutter. Leave at least 3″ (8 cm) of thread on the machine to prevent it becoming unthreaded when next used. Machine with the correct number of stitches to the inch for each fabric. Stitch-length indicators on some machines give numbers indicating this and range from about 6 to 30, others just have graduations, from 1 to 4, but it can be checked by working a row and then using a ruler to check the number of stitches to one inch. In general the thicker the fabric the fewer stitches are required.

8. Test the machine on double fabric and for best results press the row of stitching before examining.

9. Always press all machine stitching after

removing tackings to embed the stitches in the fabric and remove wrinkles, then proceed to press the process fully.

MANDARIN COLLAR   See *Collars*

MANTUA-MAKER'S SEAM
An old term to describe a join, often including gathers, which is neatened on the wrong side by hemming down one of the turnings.

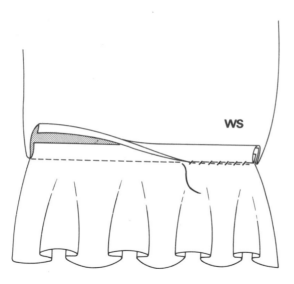

MARKING TURNINGS
Mark all turnings and any pattern symbols that will be required before removing the pattern. Choose a method suitable for the fabric, but also be realistic about the length of time to be devoted to this process according to whether you are going to carefully tailor a suit or make a child's play dress.

66

Methods

1. TAILOR TACKING (for working the stitch see under *Tailor Tacking*)

If pins have been placed well inside the edge of the pattern, the paper turnings may be quickly folded back and tailor tacks worked beside the edge of the paper. Snip the paper at neck and armhole curves to fold them back, and to tailor tack darts, cut up one side of the dart, through paper only, and fold it back. Although not the quickest method this is the most accurate way of marking turnings.

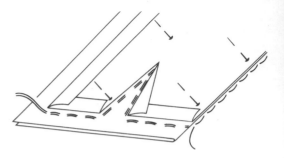

Note that tailor tacks are better not made in double loops unless the material proves extremely slippery. Make single stitches, but pick up the minimum of fabric on the needle, $\frac{1}{8}''$ (4 mm) at the most, and they will not fall out. The length of thread left on the surface will vary; make the stitches $\frac{1}{2}''$ (15 mm) long at necks and armholes but $1''$ (2·5 cm) long on straight seams. When working tailor tacks further apart than $\frac{1}{2}''$ (15 mm), make a few stitches, and then cut the threads on the surface, pulling the thread through, so leaving very short tufts of cotton. Attention to this small point will also ensure that the stitches will not fall out as there are no trailing ends to be caught in fingers, scissors, etc.

THREAD TO USE: Tacking cotton or basting cotton (e.g. Gun Basting Thread) should be used. It is made in big, inexpensive reels or cops and is especially soft to allow it to be broken easily with the fingers and so that it will not harm the fabric.

On very fine fabrics tailor tack with a fine machine darning thread (e.g. Anchor Machine Embroidery 50).

NEEDLE TO USE: A slightly coarser needle should be used than the one that would be used for hand sewing, but care should be taken not to use one that is too thick or the tufts of tailor tacks will not wedge in the fabric. Choice depends on the fabric and on which thread is used.

2. TRACE TACKING

This is a more laborious method of marking turnings as it can only be worked through one layer of fabric at a time. Use it on pieces that have been cut out in single fabric, and for marking under-collars and top collars, etc. The stitch used is ordinary tacking and if worked very close can give a continuous line where extreme accuracy is required.

3. TRACING WHEEL AND DRESSMAKERS' CARBON

Turnings may only be marked on one side of the fabric by this method, and it must always be the wrong side, as the coloured dots are not always removable. Mark two layers of fabric at once by placing two sheets of carbon paper either between the layers of fabric or one on top and one underneath, depending upon which way the fabric was folded for cutting out. A tracing wheel with very sharp teeth can cut threads in some fabrics and, in fact, as this can be a fairly hazardous method of marking turnings and quite unsuitable for some materials. The following points should be observed:

(a) Test on the wrong side of a sample piece of fabric to see if it is visible.

(b) Choose a colour carbon paper as near as possible in colour to the fabric, try not to use a direct contrast. For example, use yellow carbon on orange fabric, red carbon on pink fabric.

(c) Iron your sample to ensure that the colour does not come through to the wrong side.

(d) If a piece of marked fabric is placed against a plain piece and ironed the dots may appear on the other fabric.

(e) Never use with fabrics that have a hard or glazed surface.

(f) If used on very thick woollens the paper pattern will become torn under the pressure of the tracing wheel.

NOTE. Where sections of garment have been cut to a fold, mark this fold with trace tacking, that is, ordinary tacking. For marking other symbols, see *Balance Marks*.

METALLIC FABRICS

Plastic-coated metal is now used to add sparkle to a wide variety of knitted and woven fabrics. Styles should be simple to emphasise the splendour of the fabric. Care should be taken not to crack the threads when pressing, otherwise follow the instructions for handling Brocades.

MOUNTING

For definition of mounting and choice of fabrics, see *Lining*.

Method of Mounting

There are two procedures:

1. Cut out the garment in fabric, then, without removing the pattern, lay these pieces on the lining and cut out. Pins are unnecessary as the weight of the fabric will hold the lining in position. Mark the turnings in the fabric, remove the pattern and pin it to the lining in order to mark those turnings.

2. Cut out the lining and mark the turnings. A tracing wheel and dressmakers' carbon paper can be used on some mounting fabrics, in fact mounting on to muslin is sometimes suggested solely in order to use it as a base for carbon markings.

Remove the pattern, place it on the fabric and cut out. Turnings are not marked on these pieces.

After cutting out all pieces, remove the pattern and lay out the mounting fabric wrong side uppermost. Place each piece of top fabric with right side uppermost on to the appropriate section of mounting, taking care not to stretch or wrinkle the material. Keeping the work flat on the table, start in the centre of each piece and work basting stitches in rows up and down until the whole area is covered. Use the forefinger of the left hand to help the material on to the needle. Stitches are from 1″–2″ (2·5–5 cm) in length, with about 1″ (2·5 cm) between the rows, although this varies considerably according to the fabric being handled. These stitches should be left in position until the garment is complete, each piece being handled as one layer.

N

NEEDLES

It is important, and it makes sewing easier, to use the right size of needle for machining and for hand sewing. For hand sewing use the smallest needle possible according to the *fabric* and the *stitch* being used, and remember that a very closely woven fabric requires a finer needle than an open weave. The needle should slide fairly easily in and out of the fabric. A larger needle has a larger eye and for this reason thick threads are used with coarser needles. If a fine thread is used in a big eye it will come unthreaded. The best type of needle to use is an egg-eyed Between as it is short and, therefore, very small, neat stitches can be made.

Machine needles too should be carefully selected, and *changed according to the fabric being sewn. They should also be renewed frequently as they quickly become blunt.* A too-coarse machine needle will leave holes in the fabric and produce an unpleasant row of stitching; too fine a needle may break. Consider, too, the thickness of thread being used. See also *Threads.*

Hand-sewing Needle Sizes

Number	Fabric
9, 10, 11	Tulle, crêpe, silk, lawn, chiffon, silk, organdie and all fine fabrics.
7, 8, 9	Denim, terry cloth, flannel, velvet, jersey, corduroy, dress-wool, satin, brocade, linen, poplin, taffeta, cotton and closely woven fabrics.
7, 8	Camel hair, mohair, tweed, canvas, ticking and all heavy or thick fabrics.
8, 9, 10	Nylon, Terylene, Tricel, Dicel, Orlon, Crimplene, Courtelle, Acrilan, viscose, rayon and other synthetics.

Size of Machine Needle

Fabric	Needle Size		Stitch No. to 1 cm	Length No. to 1 cm
	British	Continental		
Silk, lawn, chiffon georgette, crêpe, fine lace, tulle, taffeta, surah, voile	9–11	70–80	14–16	5–6
Seersucker, Dicel, crêpe, Terylene, Tricel, satin, brocade, nylon jersey	11–14	90–100	12–13	4–5
Cottons, poplin, gingham, pique, needlecord, corduroy, jersey, Crimplene, velvet, rayon, duchess satin, bonded fabrics	14	80–90	12–13	4–5
Dress-weight wool, mixtures, jerseys, linen, denim, sailcloth	14–16	90–100	10–12	4–6
Worsteds, coatings, skirt-weight woollens, camel, fur fabrics, flannel	16–18	100–110	6–8	3–4

68

NYLON

Nylon was the first truly synthetic fibre; it is now greatly improved on the first cold, glassy non-absorbent fibres and is now soft and pleasant with excellent draping qualities. It is used for many fabrics including seersucker, fur fabric, brushed nylon, organza, net and lace, but it is perhaps most successful as a knitted fabric used for stockings, underwear, overalls, shirts and jersey dresses. It is easy to wash, if this is done frequently, by hand or machine and often requires no more than touching up with the iron. Sew with synthetic thread (e.g. Coats' Drima), use sharp scissors to cut, and press with a warm iron. If it proves difficult to obtain a good row of machining, place a piece of tissue paper under the work. Most nylon fabrics are somewhat transparent, so choose neat seam and hem finishes.

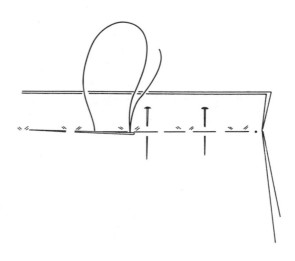

O

OPEN SEAM

With the work flat on the table to avoid stretching, tack on the fitting line, with the right sides of the material together. If pins are needed, place them at right angles to the seam edge. With curved seams lift the curved part on to the hand and pick up only the fitting line on the pin, so allowing the fabric to flute on either side of it.

Machine open seams in the correct direction (see *Direction of Stitching*). If the fabric is mounted, use a slightly larger machine stitch. Remove the tackings, press the stitching to embed it in the fabric, then press the seam open, using a method of pressing which is suitable for the material. First open the seam with the toe of the iron, then press it completely open. Snip the turnings of curved seams to allow them to lie flat.

Methods of Neatening the Open Seam

(i) BY MACHINE—STRAIGHT STITCH (use on lightweight fabrics only). After pressing open the seam, turn under the raw edges to an even width, about $\frac{1}{2}''$ (15 mm). Tack and press before stitching. Place the work under the machine with the raw edge on the underside so that the narrow turnings are held in place by the bed of the machine. Stitch as close as possible to the fold. Press the machine stitches and then trim away the raw edges to allow the seams to lie flat.

(ii) BY MACHINE—ZIG-ZAG STITCH. On lightweight fabrics turn under the raw edge and work a small zig-zag stitch over the folded edge. With medium and heavyweight fabrics work a slightly wider stitch inside the raw edge and trim the turning afterwards. On non-fraying fabrics such as jersey materials work the zig-zag over the raw edge.

If the fabric has been mounted on to a lining, the two edges tend to slip when a zig-zag stitch is worked through the two layers, causing puckering. To avoid this either tack together the turnings before stitching, or zig-zag them separately.

(iii) OVERCAST (suitable for most weights of material). On fabrics that do not fray too readily, overcast the raw edges by hand, the depth of stitch depending on the closeness of the fabric weave. Trim the raw edge just before overcasting. It may help to work a row of machining first as this will hold the edge firmly while the overcasting is worked over it. Trim very close to the machine stitches just before overcasting.

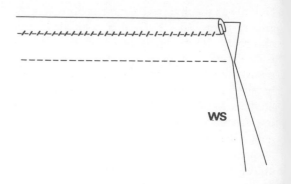

WS

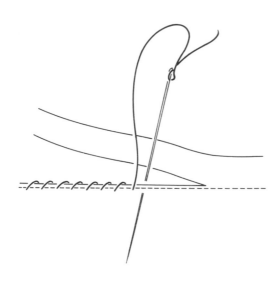

(iv) LOOPSTITCH. This takes longer than overcasting and it is not suitable for fraying materials. It prevents turnings in jersey fabrics from curling up.

(v) BINDING. This is another method of neatening turnings that takes a long time, but it is very neat and may be worth the trouble in certain circumstances. With some fabrics, such as heavy hand-woven silks, it may be the only method which will prevent fraying. The binding makes the seam more bulky, so it should not be used on thick fabrics if the garment is close-fitting. Use strips of lining cut on the cross, or commercial bias binding, and machine it to the turnings with the right sides together. Trim down the raw

edges, fold the binding over and hem it to the machining. A slightly flatter finish is produced by folding the binding right over the edge, leaving it single underneath. It is then held in position by a backstitch. (This is explained more fully under *Hems*.)

OPENINGS

1. *Continuous-strip Opening*

This is fairly strong and is often used on long sleeves. It can be made to overlap or to meet edge-to-edge. Not recommended for bulky fabrics.

METHOD

(i) Mark the opening with chalk or a row of tacking. Place it on the straight grain if possible to lessen the possibility of fraying.

(ii) Cut a strip of fabric on the straight grain equal to twice the length of the opening and about $\frac{3}{4}''$ (2 cm) wide, a little more in thicker fabrics.

(iii) Cut the slit for the opening and open it out so that it lies on top of the strip. Tack, taking $\frac{1}{4}''$ (8 mm) turnings. At the centre, the width of turning on the garment will gradually become less, but keep the turning on the strip level all along.

(iv) Machine from the garment side, being sure to catch a thread or two of fabric at the centre. Reinforce this part by machining again at this point.

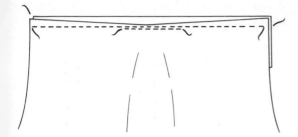

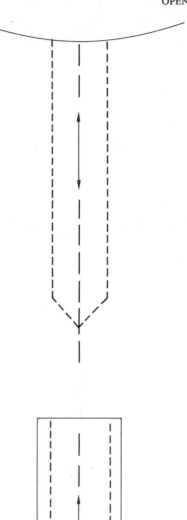

(v) Trim the turnings. Fold the strip over twice, pin and tack, starting at the centre. Finish by hemming into the machining or by machining along the edge of the strip.

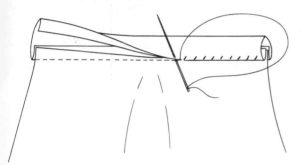

NOTE. If the opening is to be finished with machining, then begin by placing the strip to the wrong side of the garment, otherwise start on the right side.

2. *Shirt-front Opening*

This is also called a wrap and strap opening; it is conspicuous and used on shirtwaister dresses with collar and revers and also on long sleeves with cuffs.

(i) Check the pattern length carefully before cutting out. If the pattern is to be shortened it may be wise to shorten the opening to keep it in proportion.

(ii) Cut out, being especially accurate with placing the straight grain.

(iii) Do not immediately cut out the opening in the material, but mark all lines, including the centre front, with tacks. Interface the strappings and mark the turnings and centre front lines on them.

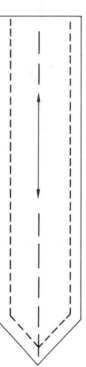

71

(iv) Stitch both strappings in position with right sides of fabric together. Sew from the *garment* side in order to keep on the tacks. Stitch from neck to bottom of strap but not across the bottom.

(vi) Stitch the bottom of the right-hand strip, taking care not to pull it off grain.

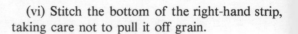

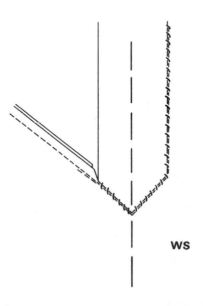

WS

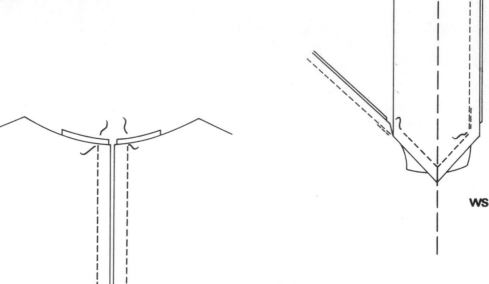

(vii) Fold over the strapping piece and hem into the machine stitches.

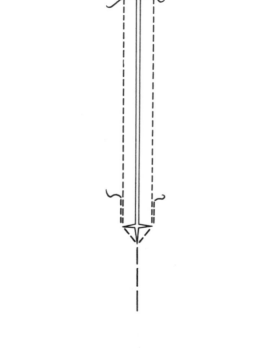

WS

(v) Cut down the centre front and snip into the corners. If the fabric frays, either reinforce with a row of small machine stitches *before* cutting or, if the fabric is suitable, back the area with a piece of soft iron-on interfacing (e.g. Vilene F2).

(viii) Complete the second side of the opening by folding the strap over and hemming into the machine stitches.

72

(ix) Finish the bottom of the under strap either by turning in the edges and slip-stitching together, or with medium and heavy fabrics it will be less bulky if the raw edges are left free, with the edge neatened with buttonhole stitch.

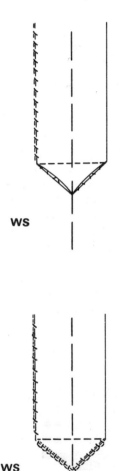

WS

WS

(x) Backstitch across the bottom of the under strip, taking the stitches through to pick up the other strapping.

3. *Other Openings*

There are other openings that are used occasionally, particularly on children's clothes, but the zip fastener has largely replaced plackets on adult clothes.

ORLON See *Acrylics*

OVERCASTING

This stitch is worked from left to right over a raw edge and is often used for neatening seams. The stitches are about $\frac{1}{4}''$ (8 mm) apart and the depth the stitch is taken into the fabric is between $\frac{1}{8}''$ and $\frac{1}{4}''$ (4 mm and 8 mm), depending upon how badly the material frays. If the material does

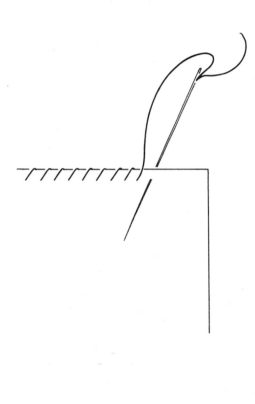

fray badly, work a row of machining first, trim the surplus edge, and take the overcasting stitches right over the machining. Use short pieces of thread, put the needle in at an angle and pull the thread through quickly to produce an angled stitch.

OVERLAID SEAM See *Lapped Seam*

OVERSEWING

This is a small strong stitch used to join two folded edges, or selvedges, together—for example: ends of straps, belts, corners of coats—and for attaching tapes and straps. Work from right to left, picking up one thread from each fold. The needle is inserted straight and the thread is pulled tight.

P

PAD STITCH

A small version of basting, pad stitch is normally worked through at least two layers of fabric and is used for attaching the interfacing of under-collars, lapels, etc., to the outer layer of fabric. It is a permanent stitch and is worked in thread which matches the material. The stitch is worked on the wrong side, on the interfacing, and shows as a small diagonal stitch, but underneath, on the right side of the fabric, it produces only a slight dent. It is essential to use an egg-eyed Between needle (see *Needles*), as these are short and enable a very small deep stitch to be taken. Insert the needle almost horizontally and work in rows about $\frac{1}{4}''$ (8 mm) apart.

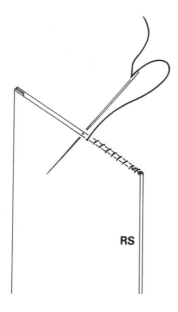

RS

PAPER PATTERNS

Commercial paper patterns are available in a uniform range of sizes. Study carefully all the measurements given for each category, for although the pattern is normally bought to correspond with the bust measurement (because it is easier to alter the hips) it may be that a different size is more suitable for other reasons. Also, figures vary so much in shape and it is often only by trial and error that the best size of pattern is found. For instance, a bust measurement of say 36", size 14 (91 cm), may be comprised of a narrow back and prominent bust, or a broad back and very small bust.

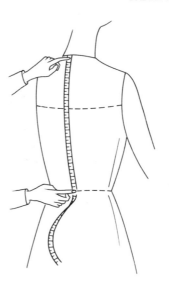

Measuring back neck to waist

Positions for measuring bust, waist and hips

The two most important measurements to check are bust and back neck to waist. The latter varies a great deal on individuals and is often not in proportion to height. With a little experience it will become obvious which size of pattern in which range corresponds most closely with the body measurements. A woman who measures 38" bust, size 16 (97 cm), but who is short, narrow-shouldered and small-boned, may well find a size 14 or 14½ pattern fits her very well because the shorter back length and smaller hips make it nearer to her size. The additional amount needed at bust level would be provided by the ease allowed in the pattern.

Ease is allowed at all points on all patterns, the amount varying according to the position on the body. For instance there is very little ease allowed at the waist, on a garment that has a fitted waist, as there is little movement, but the amount of ease allowed on the bust is approximately 3" (8 cm) (more for loose-fitting or outer garments). When checking the pattern before cutting out, only reduce the width of a pattern if it is obviously much too big or if you know from experience that you are making the correct alteration. Never reduce the pattern to your exact measurements.

The majority of women find they need to make some alteration to achieve a better fit, and it is preferable to alter the pattern before cutting out, rather than to leave it until the garment is fitted.

Size Ranges

MISSES'

Size	*6*	*8*	*10*	*12*	*14*	*16*	*18*
Bust	30½″ (*78 cm*)	31½″ (*80 cm*)	32½″ (*83 cm*)	34″ (*86 cm*)	36″ (*91 cm*)	38″ (*97 cm*)	40″ (*102 cm*)
Waist	22″ (*56 cm*)	23″ (*59 cm*)	24″ (*61 cm*)	25½″ (*65 cm*)	27″ (*68 cm*)	29″ (*74 cm*)	31″ (*79 cm*)
Hip	32½″ (*83 cm*)	33½″ (*86 cm*)	34½″ (*88 cm*)	36″ (*91 cm*)	38″ (*97 cm*)	40″ (*102 cm*)	42″ (*107 cm*)
Centre Back (Neck to Waist)	15½″ (*39 cm*)	15¾″ (*40 cm*)	16″ (*40·5 cm*)	16¼″ (*41 cm*)	16½″ (*42 cm*)	16¾″ (*42·5 cm*)	17″ (*43 cm*)

WOMEN'S

Size	*38*	*40*	*42*	*44*	*46*	*48*	*50*
Bust	42″ (*107 cm*)	44″ (*112 cm*)	46″ (*117 cm*)	48″ (*122 cm*)	50″ (*127 cm*)	52″ (*132 cm*)	54″ (*137 cm*)
Waist	34″ (*86 cm*)	36″ (*91 cm*)	38″ (*96 cm*)	40½″ (*103 cm*)	43″ (*109 cm*)	45½″ (*116 cm*)	48″ (*122 cm*)
Hip	44″ (*112 cm*)	46″ (*117 cm*)	48″ (*122 cm*)	50″ (*127 cm*)	52″ (*132 cm*)	54″ (*137 cm*)	56″ (*142 cm*)
Centre Back (Neck to Waist)	17¼″ (*44 cm*)	17⅜″ (*44 cm*)	17½″ (*44·5 cm*)	17⅝″ (*45 cm*)	17¾″ (*45 cm*)	17⅞″ (*45·5 cm*)	18″ (*45·5 cm*)

Both Misses' and Women's Patterns are made for women who are 5′ 5″ (1 m 66 cm) to 5′ 6″ (1 m 69 cm) tall

HALF-SIZES

Size	*10½*	*12½*	*14½*	*16½*	*18½*	*20½*	*22½*	*24½*
Bust	33″ (*84 cm*)	35″ (*89 cm*)	37″ (*94 cm*)	39″ (*99 cm*)	41″ (*104 cm*)	43″ (*109 cm*)	45″ (*115 cm*)	47″ (*120 cm*)
Waist	26″ (*66 cm*)	28″ (*71 cm*)	30″ (*76 cm*)	32″ (*81 cm*)	34″ (*86 cm*)	36½″ (*92 cm*)	39″ (*98 cm*)	41½″ (*105 cm*)
Hip	35″ (*89 cm*)	37″ (*94 cm*)	39″ (*99 cm*)	41″ (*104 cm*)	43″ (*109 cm*)	45½″ (*116 cm*)	48″ (*122 cm*)	50½″ (*128 cm*)
Centre Back (Neck to Waist)	15″ (*38 cm*)	15¼″ (*38·5 cm*)	15½″ (*39 cm*)	15¾″ (*40 cm*)	15⅞″ (*40 cm*)	16″ (*40·5 cm*)	16⅛″ (*41 cm*)	16¼″ (*41 cm*)

JUNIOR PETITE

Size	3	5	7	9	11	13
Bust	30½″ (78 cm)	31″ (79 cm)	32″ (82 cm)	33″ (84 cm)	34″ (86 cm)	35″ (89 cm)
Waist	22″ (56 cm)	22½″ (57 cm)	23½″ (60 cm)	24½″ (62 cm)	25½″ (65 cm)	26½″ (67 cm)
Hip	31½″ (81 cm)	32″ (82 cm)	33″ (84 cm)	34″ (86 cm)	35″ (89 cm)	36″ (91 cm)
Centre Back (Neck to Waist)	14″ (35 cm)	14½″ (37 cm)	14½″ (37 cm)	14¾″ (37·5 cm)	15″ (38 cm)	15¼″ (38·5 cm)

YOUNG JUNIOR/TEEN

Size	5/6	7/8	9/10	11/12	13/14	15/16
Bust	28″ (71 cm)	29″ (74 cm)	30½″ (78 cm)	32″ (82 cm)	33½″ (86 cm)	35″ (89 cm)
Waist	22″ (56 cm)	23″ (59 cm)	24″ (61 cm)	25″ (64 cm)	26″ (66 cm)	27″ (68 cm)
Hip	31″ (79 cm)	32″ (82 cm)	33½″ (86 cm)	35″ (89 cm)	36½″ (92 cm)	38″ (97 cm)
Centre Back (Neck to Waist)	13½″ (34 cm)	14″ (35 cm)	14½″ (37 cm)	15″ (38 cm)	15⅜″ (39 cm)	15¾″ (40 cm)

GIRLS'

Size	7	8	10	12	14
Bust	26″ (66 cm)	27″ (68 cm)	28½″ (72 cm)	30″ (77 cm)	32″ (82 cm)
Waist	23″ (59 cm)	23½″ (60 cm)	24½″ (62 cm)	25½″ (65 cm)	26½″ (67 cm)
Hip	27″ (68 cm)	28″ (71 cm)	30″ (77 cm)	32″ (82 cm)	34″ (86 cm)
Centre Back (Neck to Waist)	11½″ (30 cm)	12″ (31 cm)	12¾″ (32 cm)	13½″ (34 cm)	14½″ (37 cm)

For young children the range varies a little with different pattern companies, but most do a 'Toddlers' range.

PATTERN ALTERATIONS

Once aware of the points at which your figure deviates from the standard measurements, it takes only a moment to effect the adjustment. Alterations involve reducing the pattern by making a pleat or adding to it by cutting and inserting an extra piece of paper, so have ready pins, tape, measure, ruler, pencil and glue. Before cutting the pattern, lengthen the grain arrow so that it extends the full length of the pattern, and after making the adjustment re-draw outer edges if they have become distorted. If the shape of the pattern where a dart falls has been altered, then pin out the dart and cut across it, with it folded to obtain the correct outer edge.

Alter the Pattern, remembering the Following Points:

1. If possible, make the alteration at a place where it will not affect the shape of the pattern piece too much; for example, alter the length of a bodice pattern at some point between the armhole and the waist, if it is done higher up it will alter the armhole and affect the sleeve.

2. Try to keep each alteration fairly small, say up to 1″ (2·5 cm). It is better to make two small adjustments than one big one.

3. If you are unsure of the alteration you are proposing to make, then make a copy of the pattern and try it out on this first.

4. Ease is needed everywhere, never reduce the pattern to your exact measurements.

5. If the alteration affects a seam, remember to adjust the pattern piece that will later be joined to it.

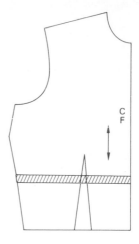

Bodice *to lengthen*
    split above waist and open out

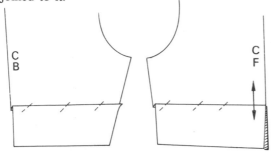

Bodice *to shorten back length*
    pleat out back bodice above waist; take similar pleat on front, but run it to nothing at centre front; straighten front edge

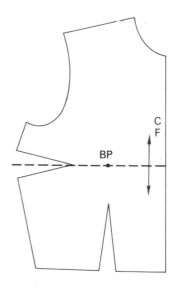

Bodice *prominent bust*
    (a) *cut through centre of bust dart to point and from there straight to centre front*

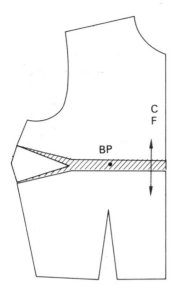

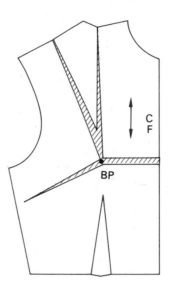

Bodice   *prominent bust*
   (b) *spread out both sections letting in required amount; keep centre front straight; redraw dart from new point in centre of inset to original base points*

Bodice   *alteration for prominent bust with dart in shoulder*

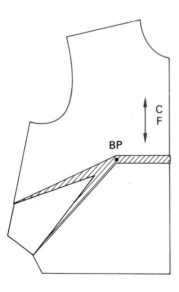

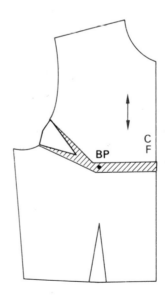

Bodice   *alteration for prominent bust with dart in armhole*

Bodice   *alteration for prominent bust with dart in armhole*

79

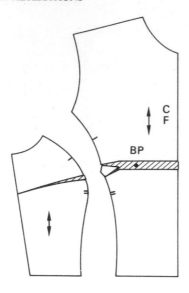

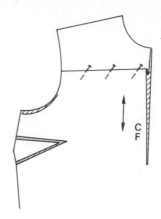

Bodice *alteration for flat chest*

Bodice *alteration for prominent bust in panel-style bodice*

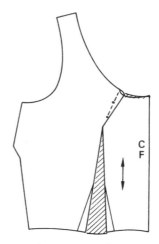

Bodice *alteration for gaping neckline*

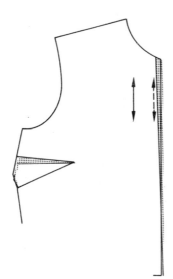

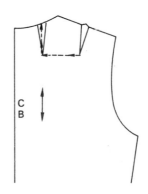

Bodice *alteration for narrow chest*
  take off a wedge-shaped piece at centre front; reduce size of dart a little if bust is also small; mark new straight grain parallel with new front edge

Bodice *alteration for rounded back*
(a) *by moving dart from shoulder to neckline; mark new dart position; fold out shoulder dart and cut from point to new line and up into neckline; dart will open in new position*

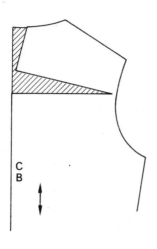

Bodice   *alteration for rounded back*
  (b) *by splitting across back and opening*

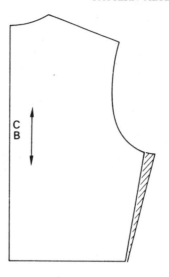

Bodice   *alteration for back broad below armhole*

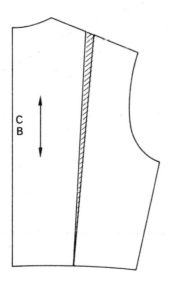

Bodice   *alteration for broad back and shoulders*

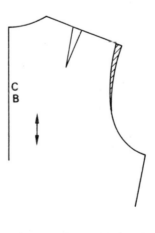

Bodice   *alteration for prominent shoulder blades*
    put a dart in the shoulder if there is not one there, or
    increase the size of an existing dart; add a little at end
    of shoulder

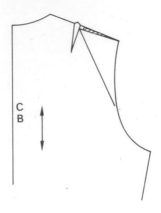

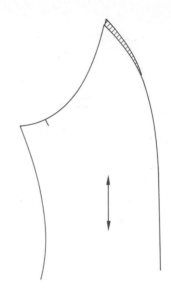

Bodice   *alteration for narrow shoulders*
cut from centre of shoulder to about halfway down the armhole; overlap a little at shoulder; redraw shoulder seam

Alteration for square shoulders—raglan sleeve

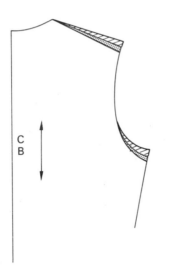

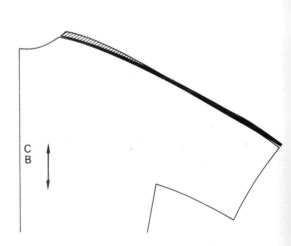

Bodice   *alteration for sloping shoulders*
slope from neckline; reduce a little at underarm to ensure sleeve fits
alteration for square shoulders
raise a little at end of shoulder; raise a little at underarm

Bodice   *alteration for square shoulders—kimono*
for sloping shoulders reduce as shown down length of sleeve

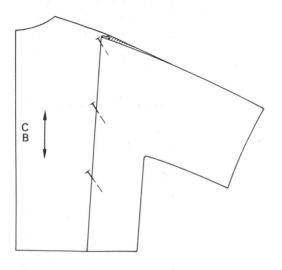

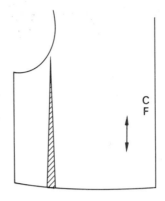

Bodice *alteration for thick waist*
split from armhole to waist and open at waist only

Bodice *alteration for narrow shoulders—kimono style*
pin out dart at shoulder running it to nothing at waist;
redraw shoulder seam; repeat on front

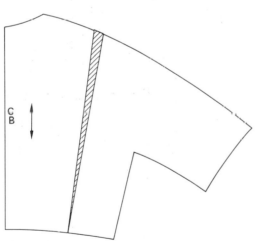

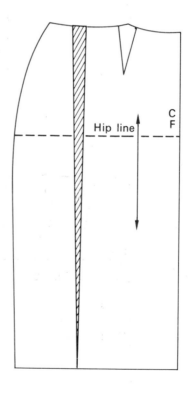

Bodice *alteration for broad shoulders and back—kimono*
style

Skirt *to alter for thick waist*

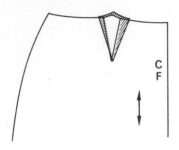

Skirt *for large stomach*
   take out bigger dart

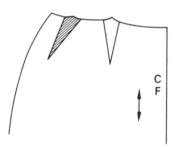

Skirt *for flat stomach*
   take dart out nearer to side seam

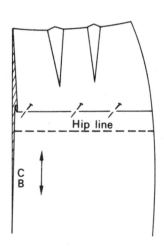

Skirt *alteration for hollow back*
   take pleat at centre back, running to nothing at side
   seam; redraw centre back line

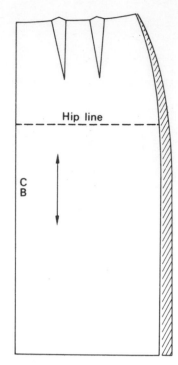

Skirt *to add a little to hip size*

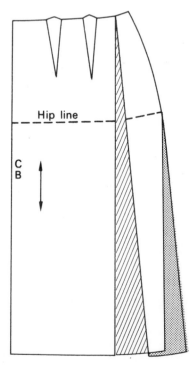

Skirt *to increase hip size by a large amount*
   split pattern and open; reduce hem-width if necessary

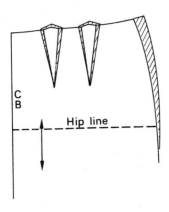

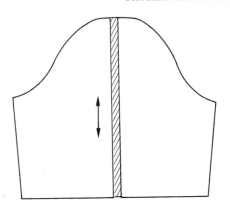

Skirt *alteration for large bottom*
  increase size of darts; add a little to side seam

Sleeve *alteration for plump top arm*

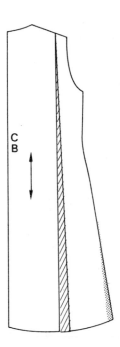

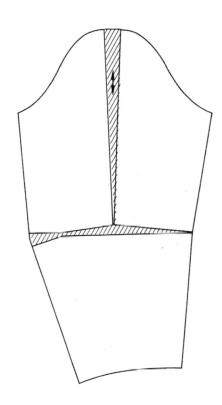

Dress *to enlarge hips on one-piece dress*
  split from shoulders to hem and open; reduce hem-width
  if necessary by taking a little off below hip line

Sleeve *to alter long sleeve for plump top arm*

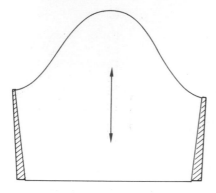

Sleeve   *for plump arm below armhole*

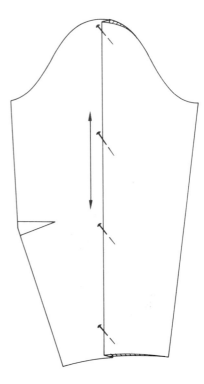

Sleeve   *alteration for thin arm*

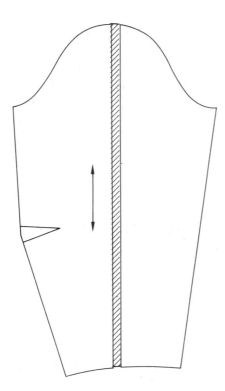

Sleeve   *to alter long sleeve for plump arm*

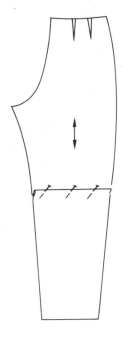

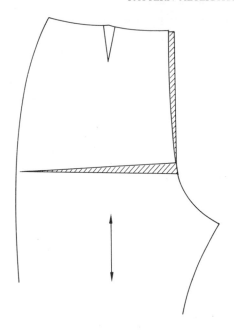

Trousers   *to shorten trouser pattern*

Trousers   *to lengthen crutch seam on trousers*
it may be necessary to straighten back seam

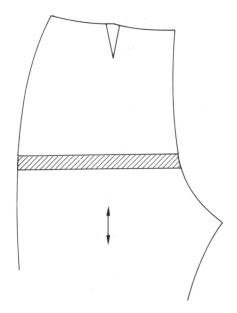

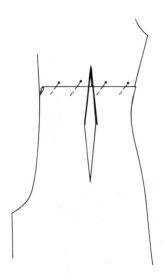

Trousers   *to lengthen crutch seam and leg length of*
trouser

To shorten culotte pattern
pin out pleat between armhole and waist

87

PILE FABRICS—Velours, Faced Cloth, Doe-skin, Camel, etc.

These are often dress or coat-weight plain-weave fabrics with a pile or nap on the right side. Cut out with the pile running down the garment as it is more pleasant to touch; this includes small pieces such as pocket flaps, cuffs, etc. Stitch the seams with the direction of the pile. Press on the wrong side with a slightly damp cloth and after pressing brush the right side of the fabric where it has been flattened.

PIPED BUTTONHOLES See *Buttonholes*

PIPED SEAMS

Cut crossway strips of material and fold in half, tack loosely and press, stretching it slightly to obtain a perfectly straight fold. Place the piping on the right side of the garment with the fold slightly over the fitting line. (It helps to put a chalk line or row of tacks $\frac{1}{8}''$ (4 mm) from the fitting line as a guide when doing this.) Turn under the edge of the other piece of material, tack and press, and then tack it down on to the piping. Top stitch by machine. If top stitching is not desired, then place the second piece of material right side down on to the piping, tack very accurately and machine.

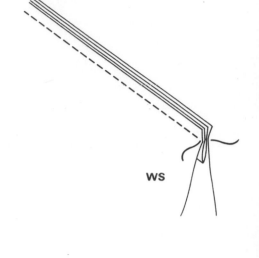

WS

For a raised effect place piping cord or crochet cotton inside the crossway strip, tack, and machine with the piping foot or zip foot on the machine. Finish as for the previous method, but again using the piping foot.

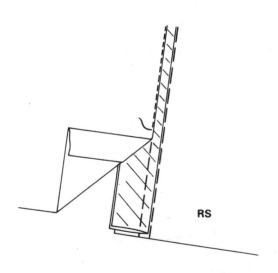

RS

RS

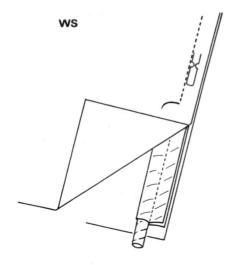

WS

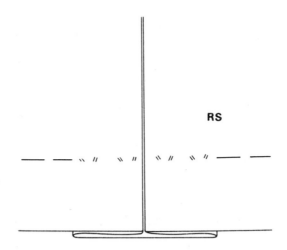

RS

avoids imprints from tackings. Fit the garment with the stitches in, only removing them when the hem is turned up.

Piping may also be made by using commercial bias binding or diagonal-weave braid folded in half.

Never press over raised piping but only up to it on each side.

PLEATS

Fold the fabric so that the pleat lines meet, tack and stitch on this line. If the pleat is to be stitched part of the way, do this work with a normal stitch and sew the remainder with a big machine stitch. Press the pleats in. This method holds the pleat firmly, produces a good knife edge and

To deal with the hem, mark the hemline using tailor tacks to mark all layers of the pleat. Remove some of the pleat stitching. Open out the hemline, turn up, press and finish in the normal way. Fold the pleat in again and hold it down with diagonal basting. Press well. Machine down

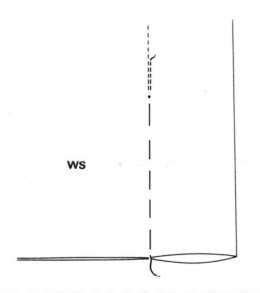

WS

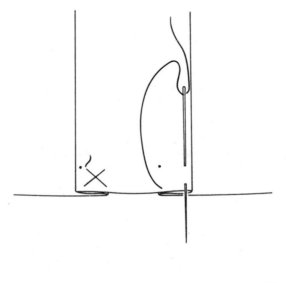

the folded edge of the pleat on the wrong side to prevent it kicking out during wear.

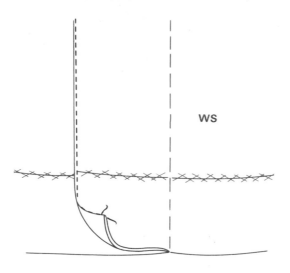

POCKETS

There are three main types of pocket: patch pockets, which are applied to the outside of the garment; seam pockets—a gap in the seam forms the pocket mouth; cut pockets—the garment is cut and the pocket bag hangs inside. All kinds must be neat and strong, and the following points should be remembered:

1. Mark positions carefully. If being made in pairs, fold the piece of garment in half and mark with tailor tacks.

2. Mark the width of the pocket accurately. (Breast pockets are $2\frac{1}{2}$"–3" (6–8 cm), others 5" (13 cm).)

3. If possible, strengthen by backing the area with interfacing, or, in the case of patch pockets, with a piece of tape at the corners.

(i) Patch Pockets

Patch pockets are best made double (either two layers of fabric or use lining or lightweight cotton for the inside). Cut the linings the same size and on the same grain as the outer pockets.

METHOD 1 (suitable for cottons and casual wear)
Machine the two layers of pocket together on the seam line, leaving a gap in the *side*. Trim turnings, snip corners and turn pocket through gap. Roll edges and tack, slip-stitching the opening. Press, tack in position on garment. Attach either by top stitching by machine, or by slip-stitching just under the edge. Make sure the top corners are very secure.

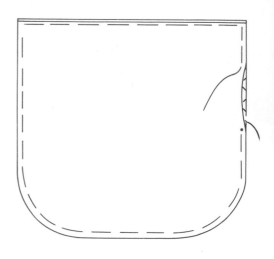

METHOD 2 (for woollens and other thick, soft fabrics)
Interface the outer pocket, trimming the edges back to the fitting line. (A lightweight iron-on interfacing such as Vilene F2 is suitable.) Fold pocket turnings over edge of interfacing and catch down, snipping where necessary to make them lie flat. Baste lining to wrong side of pocket; trim turnings down to $\frac{1}{4}$" (6 mm). Fold edge of lining under so that it is slightly back from the edge of the pocket, and slip-stitch in position. Attach pockets by machining or by slip-stitching just under the edge.

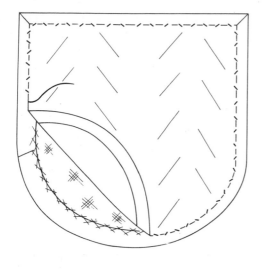

Attach the pocket-bag pieces to the turnings; press the joins open. Machine the garment seam; fasten off. Machine around the pocket bag. Press pocket in correct direction before removing tackings in mouth of pocket.

(iii) *Cut Pockets*
TYPES: (*a*) Bound—one piece. For all thin and medium-weight fabrics. (*b*) Welt, flap and jetted (or piped). For coats, etc., and all heavy fabrics. The bag is made from strong cotton or firm lining fabric.

BOUND POCKET

Cut an oblong of fabric on the straight grain. Do not attempt to curve the corners or cut it to size. Cut the oblong about 3″ (8 cm) wider than the width of the finished pocket, and make it about 12″–14″ long (30–35 cm). Centre this over the marked pocket and tack in position. Machine an oblong as for a bound buttonhole, stitching from the *garment* side for accuracy. Cut up the centre of the stitched rectangle and into the corners, push the pocket through and arrange even, neat bindings in the slit, exactly as for a bound buttonhole. Oversew the folds and press. Stitch around pocket from right side; this may be a hand prick stitch on soft fabrics, but looks neater if done by machine on cottons, etc.

(ii) *Seam Pockets* (dress, skirt, trousers)
Tack up the seam and the part that will form the pocket. Place a piece of tape, seam binding, or interfacing to the pocket mouth to prevent it stretching. Place it on the wrong side of the fabric on the piece that will become the outer part when the pocket is finished. Centre the strengthening strip over the seam line and catch it down.

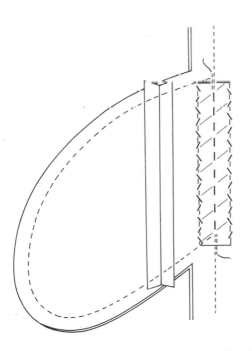

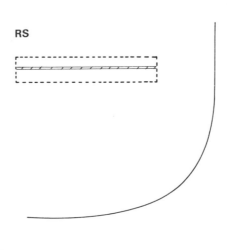

RS

On the wrong side fold the bag downwards and tack the two pieces together. Mark out a suitable size and shape for the pocket bag. (This depends on the garment; for instance, another feature of the style may mean that the bag has to be fairly short.) Stitch the bag from underneath to ensure that the machining is very close to the ends of the pocket. Trim and neaten the bag turnings. Work two rows of machining $\frac{1}{4}''$ (6 mm) apart on garments that will be subjected to hard wear.

Place pipings against the marked pocket, with the cut edges to the inside. Tack in position and machine up the centre of each piping, using the previous stitching as a guide. Make sure ends of pocket are clearly marked and fasten off ends securely. Cut from the wrong side between the rows of machining, making very long points. Push the pipings through the slit and oversew the folds together. Press. See below for attaching bag.

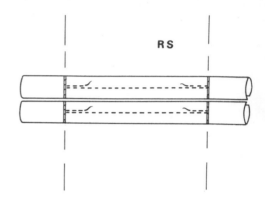

RS

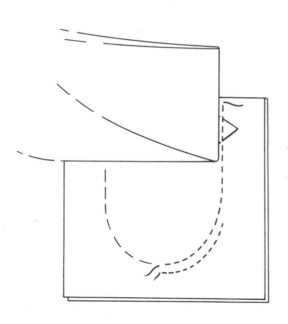

FLAP POCKET

Interface the flap and make up as for a collar, rolling out the edges and tacking and pressing to finish. Place flap to marked pocket with cut edge to the mark, and with the flap *above* the mark. Machine from end to end, fastening off ends securely. Cut a straight strip of fabric about 2'' (5 cm) wide and place it against the pocket mark so that it is below it. Machine it in place, but make sure this row of stitching is $\frac{1}{4}''$ (8 mm) shorter at each end than the flap.

PIPED OR JETTED POCKET

Cut a piece of material on the straight grain about 1'' (2·5 cm) wide, and long enough to make all pockets. Fold in half and machine it about $\frac{1}{4}''$ (6 mm) from the fold, *or* whatever width the pipings are to be. This piping may have Bondina Fusible Fleece put inside before folding (as for piped buttonholes) or it may have piping cord inserted.

RS

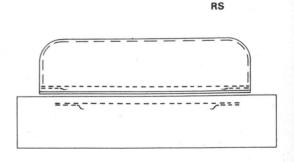

From the wrong side, cut between the rows of stitching, making long points. Fold the lower piece through the slit and use it to bind the edge, prick stitching the join to hold it down. Fold the flap down and tack above the join; tack again around the flap to keep the pocket in a closed position. For attaching bag, see below.

WELT POCKET

Make up the welt pieces as for flaps (and collars). Press and tack in position *below* the marked pocket with the cut edge against the mark.

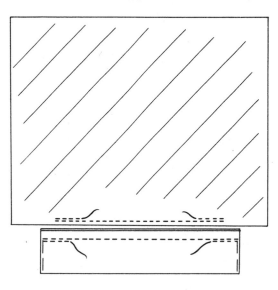

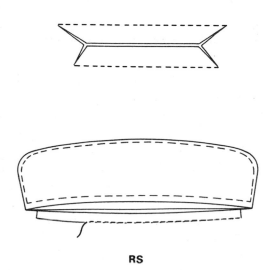

RS

The flap is held flat by a row of stitching worked about $\frac{1}{4}''$ (8 mm) below the join, this may be machining, but on soft fabrics and on coats and jackets it should be a hand prick stitch.

Machine in position, securing ends. On this pocket there is no need for a piece of fabric behind the mouth so cut a piece of pocketing (about 6″ × 6″ (15 cm × 15 cm), but not exactly to size or shape), place it to the marked pocket, above it, and machine. Make sure this row of stitching is shorter than the one attaching the welt. Cut the slit from the wrong side of the work, making long points. Push the pocket bag through the slit, press the join and let it hang downwards. Fold the welt up and tack down firmly; press. Stitch down the ends of the welt either by machine or by hand. On coats and jackets hand-stitching gives a neater appearance. For finishing of bag, see below.

RS

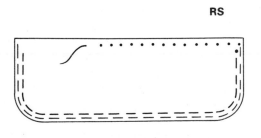

RS

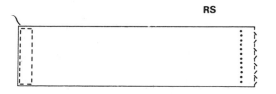

SHAPED POCKETS

Shaped pockets must be cut on the same grain as the garment so, to avoid error, lay a piece of scrap fabric on to the marked position and chalk out the shape of the welt or flap, then repeat for other pockets before cutting.

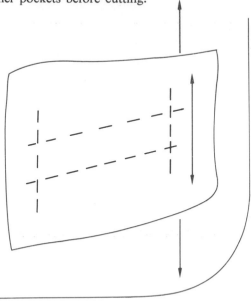

POCKET BAGS

For the under part of the bag, the one against the garment, cut a piece of pocketing of random size but making sure it is wide enough to allow for turnings. Turn under one edge and hem it in position on the wrong side of the pocket, just below the lower edge.

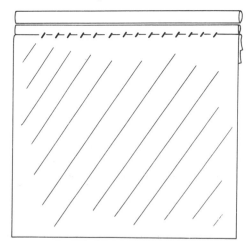

On both flap and piped pockets the mouth opens, so a piece of fabric must be placed behind the mouth of the pocket. To do this seam a piece of fabric to a piece of pocketing (random size) and press the join. Place this at the back of the pocket and machine it to the turnings above the pocket.

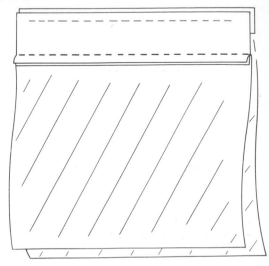

Mark out a convenient size and shape of pocket—the corners are usually rounded to prevent dust accumulating—and stitch, making sure the stitching is close to the ends of the pocket. Neaten edges of bag if fabric frays. (See sketch for bound pocket bag.)

POLYESTER FIBRES

The trade names by which polyester fibres are known include: Terylene, Crimplene, Terlenka, Dacron, Perlon. The fibre is made into a wide range of fabrics including net, suiting, lawn, overall fabrics and dress fabrics both woven and knitted. It is often blended with another, warmer, fibre such as wool or cotton, to produce a softer fabric which is more absorbent. Polyesters wash easily and drip dry and they can have permanent pleats pressed into them. For home sewing use synthetic thread (e.g. Coats' Drima) and a small needle both for hand sewing and machining. The fabrics usually fray and may also be difficult to press as they really need a hot iron, but this melts the fabric; a combination of damp cloth and medium-hot iron is usually satisfactory, but several methods should be tried out.

PREPARATION OF FABRIC

If the fabric has not been cut on a straight thread when purchased then this must be done either by snipping the selvedge and gently tearing across the width, or, on the fabrics that will not tear, by lifting one thread on a pin and pulling slightly; this will disturb the pattern sufficiently to be able to cut on the line. In the case of a printed fabric in a check or horizontal stripe the printing may not be exactly on a straight thread, so cut on the line of the pattern or the garment will appear lop-sided. Jersey fabrics are more difficult to straighten: either cut along a row of knitting or draw a chalk line at right angles to the selvedge. Pull the ends to make it level if necessary.

Next, shrink the fabric if it needs it. Many fabrics are pre-shrunk but if so they should carry some label or mark on the selvedge. The fibres most liable to shrinkage are woollens, cottons, and rayons in inexpensive ranges. Test for shrinkage by chalking a carefully measured square in the centre of the length of cloth, press with a damp cloth and leave until quite cold. Examine the fabric for bubbles around the square and also measure it. If there is the least evidence of shrinkage, press the whole length with a damp cloth on both sides, pinning the selvedges together first. Note that a steam iron is not sufficient. Washable fabrics may be shrunk by immersing them in warm water and then drip drying. If this is being done, tack the selvedges together and tack across the ends before shrinking.

Fabric is prepared for cutting out by folding with the selvedges together, with either the right or wrong sides together, and placing a few pins down the edge. Snip the selvedges if they appear tight. When fabric is folded in this way it sometimes bubbles and does not lie flat; this may be corrected by pulling from corner to corner across the puckering, or, if this is not successful, it may

have to be tacked up and immersed in water as for shrinking. Occasionally, particularly with woollen fabrics, this wrinkling can be corrected by pressing with a damp cloth.

NOTE: Never shrink crêpes or georgettes, or immerse them in water. This rule applies especially to woollens but also to some rayons. Synthetic crêpes are washable and will not be harmed, but it is unlikely that they would need shrinking treatment anyway.

PRESSING

Pressing is one of the most important aspects of sewing and it is a skill that can only be acquired through constant practice, and by handling a wide variety of fabrics. Most fabrics will withstand pressing and all will look much better for it. Inadequate pressing is the one thing which can label a garment as 'home-made'.

The equipment for pressing should be set up before beginning to sew and every process should be pressed after completion, and before proceeding to the next section. Always press each row of stitching after removing tackings as this smoothes out puckers and also helps to embed the stitches in the fabric. The actual pressing of the process is now easier. It helps to press work before machining, too. Try to keep unnecessary pressing to a minimum by keeping work on a hanger when not required.

Pressing should not be hurried, it is the use of pressure and heat (and usually moisture, too) to fold a fabric and set it in a new position. To make it lasting it is essential to spend as long as is necessary over it and also to use the correct method of pressing. A number of fabrics need special equipment, too, and these are dealt with in this book under the type of fabric, for example: lace, stretch fabrics, pile fabrics, etc. Over-pressing should be avoided, as this impairs the fabric and spoils the appearance of the garment, but this is a fairly rare mistake and is usually the result of repeated pressing *by the wrong method*. Repeated pressing by the correct method normally does no harm, as evidenced by long-lasting garments that are washed and then ironed, and men's suits, etc., that are actually pressed to improve their appearance and renew their shape.

The method of pressing must be the one that produces the best possible result in the fabric being handled, and when choosing a suitable method the type and thickness of fabric must be considered as well as the fibre or fibres from which it is made. A bare iron will adequately press some sheer or lightweight fabrics, but most other fabrics need moisture in some form. Even a cotton dress will not look perfectly finished until it has been damp-pressed. A steam iron will press some fabrics but it should be remembered that the steam is sprayed directly on to the fabric, the amount of steam cannot be varied, and the iron cannot be held still for long. By using a damp cloth, however, not only is the fabric protected from the base of the iron, but the amount of steam can be varied by wringing out the cloth or by folding it several times. When a damp cloth is used the iron must always be hot enough to convert the water in the cloth to steam very quickly (unless deliberately trying to shrink away fullness), and this may mean having the iron slightly hotter than the recommended laundering temperature. The cloth also has the effect of cooling the iron slightly. As an example of this point, synthetics such as Acrilan or Tery-lene should be pressed with a cool or warm iron if the iron is being placed directly on the fabric; if, however, dress-weight fabrics, tweeds or suitings are being sewn, this pressing will not be lasting or adequate, so a damp muslin is used with a slightly hotter iron to get a good result.

The amount of pressure exerted on the fabric will vary according to the softness of the material, and the thickness, but it also depends on the surface design and whether it is raised as with bouclé fabrics. Use wrist pressure and use the iron sharply, repeating the movement if necessary. If a damp cloth is used, remove it *immediately* the iron is raised in order to examine the work (it can be easily re-pressed while warm if it is incorrect), and also to prevent the fabric from becoming wet.

All sewing processes need pressing on the wrong side, and most will need checking, and possibly pressing, on the right side too (for example, darts). Some fabrics are best not pressed on the right side with a bare iron in case they mark or shine, but they may be protected with a dry cloth and then pressed. Finished garments, too, usually require a light all-over press on the right side.

Acquire the basic pressing equipment and then learn by experience, by pressing as wide a variety of materials and fibres as possible, and always test a scrap of the fabric *before doing any pressing on the garment.*

PRESSING EQUIPMENT

1. *Iron*

A domestic iron of reasonable weight, not too light. Keep the base plate clean after damp-pressing by wiping with a damp cloth and a little liquid soapless detergent. During use stand the iron on its heel. Make sure the flex is long enough to reach the pressing area and check the plug and lead occasionally. A steam iron is useful on some medium and lightweight fabrics, but it is not really a substitute for an ordinary iron, especially when the student of dressmaking progresses to heavier cloth and outer garments.

2. *Sleeve Board*

This is a vital piece of equipment as all processes and sections of work are pressed on it, the main weight of the work being supported below, so eliminating stretching and unnecessary creasing. Stand the sleeve board (unless it is fixed to the ironing board) on a table covered with a piece of blanket and a sheet, or use it on the ironing board. There is also the advantage that it raises the work to a more comfortable height. The sleeve board should be covered with a layer of blanket and a sheeting cover pulled tight to avoid crease marks on the work. Make several easily removable covers.

3. *Pressing Block*

Many medium and heavy-weight fabrics not only require the use of a damp cloth but it is also necessary to bang the steam well into the fabric after removing the cloth. This may be done with the back of a large heavy clothes brush or something similar, but a pressing block can easily be made from a piece of softwood. The wood must be planed and sanded very smooth on the bottom and it may be shaped into a handle on top for ease of holding. The amount of banging done with the block, and the decision as to whether the block is left in position until the work is cool, depends entirely on the type and thickness of the fabric. Avoid block imprints on the fabric by testing beforehand.

4. Pressing Cloths

A piece of muslin can be used to press a wide variety of fabrics. It can be used dry to protect fine fabrics or used damp. Where more moisture is needed for thicker or more difficult fabrics, fold it double or into four. It can also hold varying amounts of water according to how tightly it is wrung out. For shrinking away fullness, have it fairly wet and folded into four or eight layers, place it on the work and hold the iron lightly on it. A damp muslin can also be used to rub along seams, etc., on fabrics which can be pressed dry in the normal way, but need a little moisture to obtain a good finish on sewing processes.

Coatings, suitings, worsteds, tweeds, etc., may need the use of a thicker damp cloth for pressing. Use a piece of sheeting for this, preferably not new. A piece of old sheet or pillow case is best as it can be wrung out well. Never use this thick cloth when pressing fine or medium-weight fabrics as it holds more water and would tend to make the material wet.

5. Soap

Rub dry laundry soap on the back of pleats or trouser creases and when pressed the soap will help the creases to set.

6. Pressing Pads

An egg-shaped pad is useful for pressing shaped areas, collars, armholes, etc., and a flat oblong pad can be used for pressing sleeves, but a good substitute is a folded Turkish towel. Make a seam roller by wrapping a rolling pin in a tea towel or make a selection of different-sized

rollers from pieces of broom handle, dowelling, pencils, knitting needles, etc. Cover with wadding or plastic foam sheeting and then a layer of cotton sheeting.

The use of pressing rollers should be kept to a minimum as only the row of stitching is pressed and it is not possible, due to their shape, to exert any pressure on the work, and this can result in the work appearing inadequately pressed.

Pressing the Completed Garment

PREPARATION:
1. Make sure you have plenty of time, it is a slow job.
2. Do not press just before you want to wear it, do it the day before.
3. Make sure you have the iron close to the outlet socket in order to reach all parts easily.
4. Have everything ready, including pressing pads, towel, clothes brush, coat hanger, scissors for odd threads.

ORDER OF PRESSING:
(i) Sleeves and cuffs.
(ii) Front edges up to collar.
(iii) Collar.
(iv) Any other small parts: pockets, etc.
(v) Shoulders and sleeve heads.
(vi) Main body of garment.
(vii) Run a cool iron over the lining.

Methods of Pressing, Various Processes

PRESSING DARTS
Having shaped a dart carefully to the figure it is important not to flatten out this shape during pressing. After pressing the machine stitches flat, open out the work and arrange it on the sleeve board with the dart stitching running straight along the board and the point just reaching the end of the board. This allows the shaped part of the fabric to hang below the board and it will therefore not be flattened by the pressing. At the same time the main part of the fabric is being supported by the table below the sleeve board. Settle the dart in its position by lightly

pressing it over to one side (the bulk of the fabric lies towards the centre or downwards), or cut the fold and open it, or flatten it like a box pleat. Proceed to press the dart by a method of pressing suitable for the fabric. Most fabrics require the use of a cloth, and this should be held upright at the point of the dart while manipulating the iron with the right hand; this enables you to see the work and to ensure that pressing is not done beyond the end of the dart stitching. After allowing it to cool, turn the work over and, placing it back on the board, *do not hold it up*, examine the line of the dart. There should not be a pleat along the stitching line nor a sudden tuck or bulge at the point. It may be necessary to lightly press the right side to obtain a good finish.

PRESSING SEAMS

After pressing the stitching, place a short section of the seam on the sleeve board and open it with the fingers. If the fabric is springy open the seam with the toe of the iron. Press the seam open, working in the same direction as the stitching was done, that is, from hem towards neck. Press the seam firmly but sharply by the method chosen for the fabric. Take care that the section pressed is cool before moving on to the next part. Many fabrics require the use of the pressing block to bang in steam after removing the damp cloth, in order to obtain a really flat finish. When cool turn the work over, without holding it up, and examine the right side, pressing lightly if necessary.

Curved seams should be pressed towards the sharpest part of the curve from each direction, snipping the turnings if necessary. This applies when pressing the hip curve of skirt seams as well as the more shaped seams of a panel line or princess style.

If pressure has left turning imprints these can usually be removed by running the iron along under the turnings, *except* in the case of rayons and silks, and these should be pressed over a pad or seam roller, or avoid imprints by placing strips of spare material or paper under the turnings before pressing.

PRESSING EDGES

Garment edges need a firm press, especially where a separate facing has been attached. Place sections of the edge on the sleeve board and press firmly, taking care not to allow the weight of the work to stretch the edge.

PRESSING SLEEVE HEADS

This is done after the sleeve is set into the armhole. Turnings are not snipped and not trimmed, but left at the full width and pressed towards the sleeve. In this way the sleeve and armhole turnings provide support for the head of the sleeve, giving it a good shape. Place a folded towel inside the armhole and, holding this in the left hand, use the right hand to press the sleeve join, placing the damp cloth over part of the seam, pressing with the toe of the iron, removing the cloth and moving to the next part of the seam, and so on.

PRESSING SLEEVES

Short sleeves can usually be pressed on the sleeve board, but avoid creases in long and three-quarter sleeves by using a pressing pad. If a sleeve pad is not available, fold a small towel or piece of blanket to a flat oblong and slide it into the sleeve. Press the sleeve, turning it to reach all parts.

PRESSING COLLARS

Always keep the curved shape of the collar by pressing it in sections after it has been attached to the garment. First, lift the collar and press the neck-join from underneath the collar, then press the outer edge of the collar. Finally fold the collar into its rolled position and place it over a sleeve board or over a towel folded into a cube shape, and press up to the roll of the collar but not over it.

P.V.C. FABRICS

The P.V.C. material widely available by the yard is made by applying a plastic finish to a fabric such as cotton. Where cotton is the backing fabric, the result is slightly more rigid than the more expensive ones, which are made from plastic bonded to a jersey backing. P.V.C. needs special care and the following hints may be found helpful:

1. Choose a simple style with raglan or kimono sleeves, as curves are difficult to deal with.

2. Fit the pattern before cutting out, as any unpicking of stitches leaves holes in the fabric.

3. The pattern may be attached to the fabric with sticky tape for cutting out; use it for assembling for fitting in place of tacking.

4. Mark essential turnings with pencil on the wrong side.

5. Use eight to ten stitches to one inch (2·5 cm) when machining, and a medium needle. Sprinkle the machine bed with talcum powder and rub the needle with an oily cloth occasionally. Avoid too much hand sewing; use instead either Bondina Fusible Fleece or Jiffytex for sticking hems. A certain amount of machining can be done on the jersey-backed fabrics as these are more supple. Make piped or machine buttonholes.

6. Avoid top stitching where possible as it is very difficult to prevent the foot sticking to the fabric.

7. Curves are difficult and turnings have to be well snipped before machining.

8. Press on the wrong side with a steam iron, or warm iron, but always cover the work with a pressing cloth.

9. Use 'Velcro' fastener for openings, attaching belts, tabs, etc., although if using the 'leather-look' P.V.C. an invisible Alcozip is easy to insert.

R

REINFORCEMENTS

There are a number of positions which require some strengthening or supporting so that the garment wears well.

1. Raglan seams. Part or all of a raglan seam is cut on the cross and it is advisable to stitch shrunken tape to the fitting line to prevent the seam losing its shape.

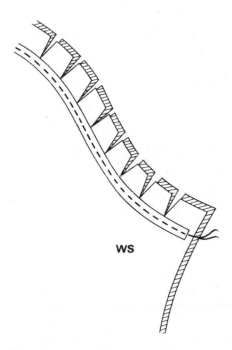

WS

2. Shaped seams often need clipping right to the fitting line, so reinforce the sections before clipping either by working a row of machining or by sewing a piece of tape on the fitting line. Note that the tape will not be clipped.

3. A kimono sleeve which is a type cut in one with the bodice allows only restricted arm movement and is therefore subject to strain. The use of a gusset will give more room (see *Gussets*), but if this is not desirable then strengthen the underarm seam by stitching tape to the fitting line.

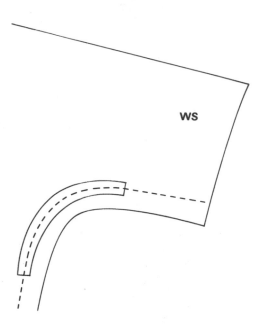

4. When sewing buttons on to loosely woven materials, either put a piece of linen in position between the facing and outer fabric (this is in addition to the interfacing) or place a piece of folded tape at the back of the fabric (not for coats and jackets or in positions where tape would be visible). On heavy-duty garments like raincoats or anoraks sew a tiny button on the back as a reinforcement.

5. Pleats. Where a series of pleats are subjected to strain, reinforce them by sewing a piece of tape in position across the top of the pleats on the wrong side.

6. Reinforce the crutch seam of slacks or shorts by stitching a piece of tape into the seam.

REVERSIBLE FABRICS .

These are made by joining two layers of fabric, usually woollen. The more expensive ones are joined by a random thread which runs between the two fabrics—this can be snipped, enabling the layers to be parted; others are joined by adhesive and cannot be separated. Truly reversible fabrics are of comparable quality on both sides and can be made into garments that can be worn both ways, but many have a slightly inferior quality brushed wool on one side and these are used for casual unlined garments.

These fabrics are all fairly thick, so avoid unnecessary bulk by not using facings or turning hems.

To make a reversible garment:
1. Choose simple loose-fitting styles with raglan or kimono sleeves.
2. Use welt seams.
3. Bind all edges, collar, hems, front edges, sleeves, etc., with wide diagonal-weave wool braid.
4. Make patch pockets.
5. Use frog fastenings and toggle buttons or use rouleau or braid loops and a set of buttons on each side.

Separating Reversible Fabrics
If the fabric can be parted, treat as follows:
DARTS: Split the two layers and make the darts in each piece separately; split them and press them open before tacking the layers together.

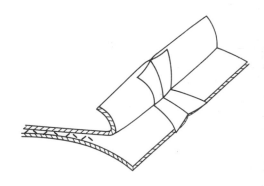

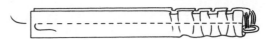

SEAMS: Separate the layers, join two edges together, press open. Turn the other two in towards each other and slip-stitch together. Press well.

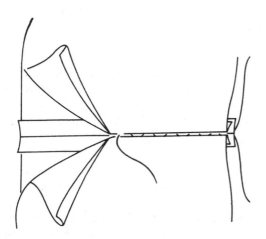

HEMS, FRONT EDGES, COLLAR EDGES, SLEEVES, ETC.: Split the layers and turn the edges in to meet each other; slip-stitch together.

BUTTONHOLES: Separate the two layers and make bound buttonholes in one side; finish in the usual way, using the other layer as a facing.

It will help in handling the fabric to slip a piece of Bondina Fusible Fleece between the layers before sewing up again.

ROULEAU

Rouleau is a narrow tube of fabric made as narrow as the fabric will allow (this depends on thickness) and made plump by leaving the turnings inside. Lengths of rouleau can be made from any fabric, but it is most successful in jersey fabrics as these stretch and roll well, do not fray and do not split when turned through.

To make Rouleau

Cut a length of fabric on the cross grain four times the finished width. If using a woven fabric, iron Bondina Fusible Fleece on to the wrong side and remove the paper backing. Fold the strip in half, tack and machine up the centre, using a slight zig-zag stitch if possible. Trim one turning

down by $\frac{1}{16}''$ (2 mm). Push a bodkin or elastic threader into the end (or use a tapestry needle or rouleau needle—a long thin one with a large eye). Sew the eye of the bodkin firmly to the turnings of the rouleau and ease it through. Jersey rouleau will not require pressing, but press others lightly.

ROULEAU LOOPS

Many paper patterns will have the size and shape of each loop printed on the pattern. If so, tack the rouleau to it, with the join to the inside of the curve, lift the pattern on to the garment section and machine along the fitting line to anchor the loops. Tear away the paper and proceed to attach facing in the usual way. If you are planning your own loops draw one on a piece of paper and then copy it several times. Tack the loops to the paper and attach as described above.

For continuous rouleau loops cut a strip of paper the length of the opening, fold it into squares and draw a loop on each square. Tack the rouleau to the paper, winding it backwards and forwards. Snip halfway through the rouleau at the bend to allow it to lie flat. Attach as described above.

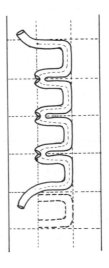

13. Insert zips by hand or use invisible zips (e.g. Alcozip).

14. Press with the toe of the iron on the wrong side only to avoid imprints. Where it is necessary to press over a double edge, place another piece of fabric under it where possible, for example, open seams. *Do not overpress.*

S

SATIN-WEAVE FABRICS

A satin effect can be produced on the right side of many fabrics by a diagonal weave. Satin-weave fabrics are made from cotton and viscose rayon as well as silk, acetate and Terylene. These fabrics should be cut with pattern pieces all one way, but apart from that it is only the soft rayon and silk dress satins that may be difficult to handle and the following rules apply:

1. Fit pattern to avoid unpicking.

2. Cut all pieces one way on the fabric as light catches it differently. Use needles instead of pins.

3. Interface with organdie or organza.

4. Tack up with machine embroidery thread.

5. Mount on fine taffeta or Jap silk.

6. With some types of satin, needle marks may show, so in this case it is best to mount on linings by tacking around the edges rather than by basting all over.

7. Use open seams and avoid top stitching on the garment.

8. Use pins only in seam allowances as the fabric marks easily.

9. Stitch with synthetic thread (e.g. Coats' Drima) to avoid puckering and use fifteen to twenty stitches to the inch (seven to eight to 1 cm). For hand sewing, use silk thread and a No. 9 or 10 hand-sewing needle.

10. To prevent the two layers slipping, place a few pins across the seam at intervals.

11. Avoid buttonholes; use loops instead.

12. Take care when turning up hems not to press over the raw edges.

SEAMS—Basic Information, Choice and Types
A seam is a neat method of joining up pieces of material, some seams being fitting seams, for example, shoulder and side seams, while others are decorative or form style lines.

When choosing a Seam, consider the Following:
1. THE STYLE. Decide whether the style is suitable for decorative seams or whether the design demands seams which are plain in appearance.

2. THE POSITION OF THE SEAMS. Seams which emphasise the bust or hips should be smooth.

3. THE WEIGHT AND THICKNESS OF THE FABRIC. With bulky fabrics choose seams which do not involve several layers of material and if possible those where some of the bulk can be cut away.

4. THE NATURE OF THE FABRIC. If the material frays, leave wide seam allowances when cutting out, and choose seams that can be neatened easily, for example a french seam on chiffon and georgette.

5. THE TYPE OF GARMENT. Double-stitched seams are strong for casual clothes and children's wear.

Main Types of Seam
1. OPEN SEAM. This is the most common seam used in dressmaking and tailoring. It is flat, not bulky, and it is easy to establish a good stitching line at fittings. Careful pressing is important (see *Pressing*). It is suitable for almost any fabric and is used on all adults' outer clothes.

2. MACHINE FELL OR FLAT FELL SEAM. This is a strong seam with two rows of stitching showing on the right side. It is slightly bulky, suitable for play clothes, jeans, pyjamas, shirts, shirt blouses, cotton slacks, denim or linen, safari jackets, dungarees. Use on thin and medium-

thickness fabrics with a plain crisp finish, not for jersey fabrics, woollens or those with raised patterns.

3. FRENCH SEAM. This is a neat seam enclosing the raw edges but involving four layers of fabric and so is only suitable for thin fabrics, such as nylon, cotton, thin rayons, chiffon and other transparent fabrics. Use for loose, washable garments such as children's clothes, nightwear, underwear and blouses. It is not suitable for curved or shaped seams, or for fitted garments, as the first row of stitching made is not on the fitting line.

SELVEDGE

This is the non-fraying edge of fabric; it some-times has holes along it where it has been gripped by machinery. In cases where it is difficult to determine the right and wrong side of the fabric, close examination of the selvedge may provide the answer. Snip the selvedges every few inches before cutting out to enable the fabric to lie flat. When cutting pattern pieces near the selv-edge, leave a wide turning so that it may be cut off when the seams are neatened; leaving a long section of selvedge inside a garment can cause a puckered seam.

SHEER FABRICS

Sheers include ninon, chiffon, and georgette and can be made from nylon, rayon, Terylene or silk. Styles should be full, as fabrics lend themselves well to gathers, draping, frills and flares. They fray badly and are difficult to handle, so it may be helpful to observe the following points:

1. Fit the pattern before cutting out to avoid making alterations in the fabric.

2. Using needles or fine steel pins, pin the fabric to tissue paper and cut out tissue paper and fabric together.

3. Tack and machine all parts on tissue paper, tearing it away after sewing. Machine with tissue on underside to cover teeth of feed.

4. Use synthetic thread (e.g. Coats' Drima) for seams, and No. 50 thread or machine em-broidery thread for hems and edges where there is little strain during wear.

5. Use a No. 8 or 9 sewing needle and a fine machine needle No. 11 English (90 continental) and fifteen to twenty stitches to the inch.

6. Make narrow french seams or zig-zag raw edges together and trim to $\frac{1}{4}''$ (8 mm).

7. In chiffon fabrics avoid buttonholes. In-stead use rouleau loops and small covered buttons or make some rouleau into a tie. Use no interfacing and avoid facings wherever possible.

8. It is best not to attempt to insert a zip into chiffon. Put the zip into the underdress and either leave the chiffon as a slit opening or attach it by hand afterwards in a few places.

9. Press with the toe of a cool iron.

10. Finish edges with a double bind, a double-stitched hem, hand rolling or shell edging. Shell edging can be done with a zig-zag machine stitch.

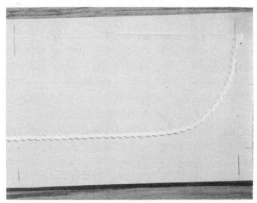

Shell edging worked on a Bernina Record

SILK

Silk, the luxury fabric, should be made into luxurious garments, sewn carefully and treated gently. Silk, one of the oldest fibres, can be from cultivated or wild silkworm cocoons; the latter produces a fibre of uneven thickness. It is made into such fabrics as crêpe de chine, organza, velvet, shantung, tussore, brocade, damask, faille, foulard, georgette, chiffon, cloqué, Jap, marquisette, matelasse, ottoman, satin. Silk fibres should not be damp-pressed, nor should they be pressed on the right side with a bare iron.

SLEEVES

Fitting

Test the fit and hang of sleeves by slipping one on to the arm when fitting the garment and pin it at the sleeve head, matching the sleeve point to the shoulder seam. The grain should hang straight and there should not be any wrinkling across the top of the arm or radiating from the underarm. If it looks satisfactory tack both sleeves into the garment and re-fit. Faults can be corrected by undoing tackings (sometimes on part of the sleeve only) and re-pitching the sleeve, more to the front or back of the garment, until it looks right. Remove lateral creases by releasing more length at the sleeve head. A droopy sleeve may need lifting more at the sleeve head. Re-tack and re-fit before stitching.

Elbow shaping, for example darts, should be at elbow level or slightly below for comfort. Long sleeves should be made a comfortable length for the individual.

Making up—See also *Double Sleeves*

Stitch sleeve seams from armhole to wrist and press seams open. Loose-lined long (or three-quarter length) sleeves are made as follows:

Make up and press the sleeves. Make up the linings a little bigger than the sleeves by stitching just in the turning. Press these turnings either open or both in the back of the sleeve. Turn the sleeve inside out and with the lining right side outwards slip the lining on to the sleeve. Match up the seams and darts and, holding the sleeve by sliding it on to the left arm, work a row of basting along the seams to hold them together. Continue working rows of basting around the sleeve, leaving several inches free at the top and bottom, until about four or five rows are in position. Turn up the hems on the sleeves and press and catch down. Turn under the linings so that the edges are $\frac{1}{2}''$ or $\frac{3}{4}''$ (15 or 20 mm) back from the lower edge of the sleeve. Turn under so that there is a little ease in the length, and fell down. Press the sleeves before setting in.

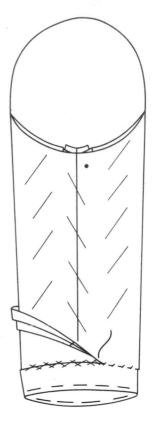

SETTING IN SLEEVES

Both the bodice and the sleeves should be made up and pressed so that setting in the sleeves is one of the final processes. This reduces unnecessary creasing.

Proceed as follows:

With bodice and sleeves right side outwards, place the sleeve seam to the bodice underarm seam (or match balance marks if there is no underarm seam) and pin. Pin the sleeve to the armhole for about 3″ (8 cm) on either side of this point. Take care not to stretch the sleeve at this stage as the whole section is on the cross grain. Move to the other sleeve and pin the underarm section. It is advisable to do this while still having the feel of the way the fabric was manipulated.

Put the left hand into the bodice and take hold of the sleeve head, hold the balance mark of the sleeve to the shoulder seam and, without letting go, pull it through to the wrong side and place a pin across the turnings. It is only the unattached sleeve head that is pulled through and then folded back over the armhole turnings so that the sleeve, the bigger piece of fabric, is on the top. Holding the work in the left hand, spread out the fingers under the armhole turnings and then pin the sleeve head to it. Place all pins across the turnings and pick up only the fitting line; this allows the turnings to flute, but there should be no actual folds of fabric under the pins. The sleeve head is, however, bigger than the armhole so a certain amount of manipulating is necessary to even out this ease to prevent it pleating. If, as

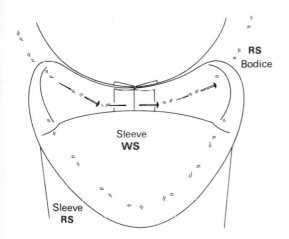

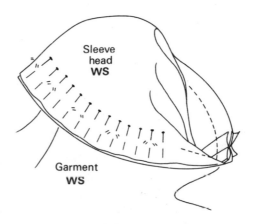

If the balance marks on the sleeve and armhole do not match, do not force the fabric; the marks may be inaccurate due to alterations made at a fitting, although of course new balance marks can be inserted at fittings. NOTE: If sleeve is loose-lined then set in only the outer sleeve, fold the lining back out of the way. If the sleeves are mounted then treat as one and set in both layers together. Tack these underarm sections and fasten off the tacking.

happens with some synthetics, it is not possible to set the sleeve smoothly, remove the pins and run a row of machine stitching along the fitting line (do not undo the underarm), and this will have the effect of tightening the sleeve head. Do not gather the sleeve head unless gathered sleeves are in fashion. With woollen fabrics, excess ease may be shrunk away after pinning by placing a damp cloth over this part and holding a warm iron over it. Tack the sleeve heads in position, remove the pins and fit the garment.

Stitch the sleeves in, either using double thread and a backstitch (the most satisfactory as the work can still be held over the hand) or machining very slowly and carefully around the armhole. Alternatively, for additional strength, a row of machining can be placed on top of the backstitching.

Remove tackings; press turnings towards armhole. Do not trim or snip turnings. See *Pressing Sleeves*.

Finishing Armholes

Finish raw edges according to the fabric either by overcasting, zig-zagging stitch on the machine, or by binding. A neat finish is obtained by working a row of machining $\frac{1}{2}''$ (2·5 cm) away from the sleeve stitching and then trimming and overcasting.

Lined sleeves are finished by stitching the bodice lining to the turnings. Use a tacking stitch, but use the thread being used to sew the garment. Take the edge of the sleeve lining, turn it under (less than a full turning to allow plenty of ease in the length) and pin it to just cover the tackings. Tack and fell in position. Because of the nature of lining fabrics it will not be possible to ease away fullness as when setting in sleeves, but tiny tucks over the sleeve head are permissible.

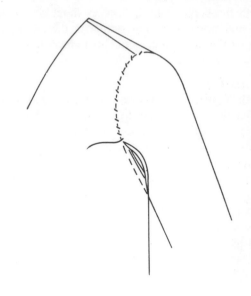

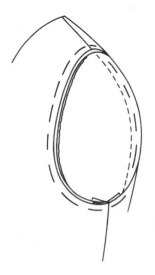

SLIP-STITCH

Sometimes referred to as ladder stitch, this is used to join two folded edges—for example, ends of straps or ties, hem corners on coats, jackets, blouses. Work the stitch by taking a small amount of fabric on the needle in one fold and then a small amount in the opposite fold, pulling the thread fairly tightly.

SLIP TACKING

(*a*) This is a method of marking turnings (also called thread marking or trace tacking) through a single layer of material only, and is often employed on slippery fabrics or those unsuitable for tailor tacks or where a pattern piece has been cut from single material. It can be worked before the pattern is removed by placing a piece of cardboard between the two layers of material to work the first row; the pattern then has to be removed and repinned to the under piece.

(*b*) This can also refer to a method of tacking on the right side where pieces have to be joined very accurately. It is useful for matching checks and also for tacking seams when a garment has been fitted and pins left in to indicate alterations.

SLOT SEAM

This looks almost like an inverted pleat when finished; the backing may be a contrasting colour or checked or striped fabric and may be cut on the straight or cross grain. First tack (or machine with a big stitch) an open seam and press. Cut backing strips of the desired width and mark their centres with tacks or chalk. Place backing in position and tack up the centre to secure in the correct position, then tack raw edges down. Top stitch from the right side and even distance from the centre. Press and then remove the centre stitching.

STITCHES See under name of stitch

STRAP SEAM

This is a bulky seam not suitable for heavy-weight fabrics. Place wrong sides of work together and stitch on the fitting line. Press open and trim turnings to about $\frac{1}{4}''$ (8 mm). Cut a strip of fabric (possibly a contrasting colour) on the straight grain the desired width of the strap plus turnings. Fold under turnings, tack and press. Mark centre of strap with chalk or tacks.

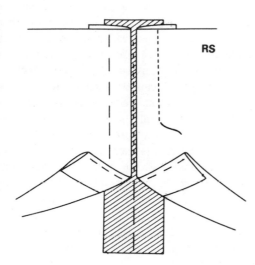

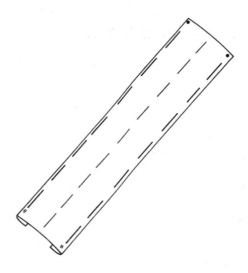

STAY STITCHING

This is a row of machine stitches worked just outside the fitting line, that is, nearer to the raw edge, to prevent stretching. It is necessary to insert this stitching if the fabric is very loosely woven or particularly liable to stretch and go out of shape. Use it at places where the weight of the garment may cause the stretching or where the edge is cut on the cross—for example, Vee neckline, waist of skirt cut on the cross. Although the stay stitching is normally left in the finished garment, it is a precaution taken to prevent stretching only during handling and making-up, stretching will not occur once the process is complete. See under *Reinforcing* for details of strengthening parts of garments.

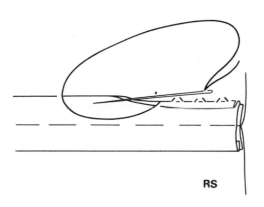

Place it centrally down the seam join, tack and top stitch or slip-stitch in position.

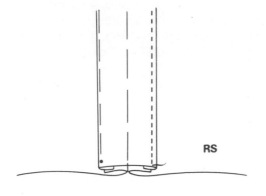

RS

STRETCH FABRICS

It is possible to buy stretch fabrics by the yard and these include denim, linen-weave rayons, towelling and sailcloth; and another type where the elastomer threads have been interwoven with the yarn include worsteds for slacks and luxurious silk stretch fabrics. They are all comfortable to wear as they give with the body.

1. Determine the direction of the stretch and then cut out to the best advantage; this is normally with the stretch running from waist to hem.

2. Pins are sometimes difficult to insert unless they are very sharp, and it is essential to use large sharp scissors.

3. Use either silk thread or synthetic thread (e.g. Coats' Drima), both of which are slightly elastic and will give with the fabric. If possible use a slight zig-zag machine stitch and a fairly loose top tension. Use ten to fifteen stitches to 1″ (four and a half to seven to 1 cm).

4. Press lightly with a steam iron on the wrong side.

5. If a lining is needed, use jersey nylon which also gives a little.

T

TACKING

A temporary stitch used for joining pieces of fabric which is removed after the permanent stitch has been worked. It is important that tacking be quickly and easily removed without damage to the fabric. Use tacking thread; it is weak and easily broken with the fingers. Machine embroidery thread can be used on fine fabrics such as silks, chiffon, velvet, etc., as it is very fine and will not pull threads in the material. Uneven tacking (long and short stitches) is slightly stronger and is used when tacking up for a fitting. Tacking with an occasional backstitch is used for setting gathers or in any position where the layers of fabric are likely to slip.

Begin with a knot (for ease of removal later) and place work flat on the table wherever possible. End with one backstitch, or two if garment is to be fitted.

TAILOR TACKING—Thread Marks, Mark Stitches

These are temporary marking stitches put in after cutting out and before removing the pattern, and used to indicate accurately seam allowances, darts, balance marks and any special features such as pocket and buttonhole positions. Work the stitch through the two layers of material, using a long piece of tacking thread double without a knot. Lay the work flat out on the table and pick up the minimum of material on the needle, helping the work on to the needle with the left forefinger.

RS

Tailor tacking   *small stitches, long threads*

Tailor tacking   *snip loops*

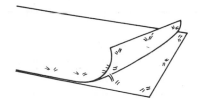

THREADS

Using the correct thread and needle for each stitch and each fabric in sewing not only makes the job much easier but the result is more professional. The mistake often made by the amateur is that she uses too big a needle and too coarse a thread, and a good general rule to follow is to use the finest thread possible for the fabric and the smallest needle (of the correct type) for the thread chosen (see also *Needles*). When buying thread, undo the thread from the reel and lay it on the fabric. Choose a slightly darker shade for a perfect match, and with mixtures try several colours and choose the most inconspicuous when laid.

A selection of threads

1. Mercerised cotton (e.g. Coats' satinised) is available in No. 40 thickness for most general sewing by hand and machine, and in No. 50 which is finer and will produce less obvious stitches. Mercerised thread is available in an almost unlimited range of colours. Threads made from vegetable fibres have a tendency to dry out over a period of time, which can cause them to break easily, so it is always wise to purchase new thread for each garment.

2. Cotton (e.g. Coats' Six Cord in Nos. 24, 30, 40, 60) is a dull-surfaced thread used for all household jobs and for sewing plastics, leathers, suede and imitation leathers. The range of colours is limited.

3. Synthetic thread. There are several threads available made from synthetic fibres which are used for stitching fabrics made from synthetic fibres. The thread is fairly elastic and will give with the fabric. Hand sewing may be found difficult with these threads as they tend to twist up and the cut end may unravel (although the latter can be rectified by re-cutting the end of thread at an angle).

There is one thread, however, that can be used on all types of fabric, both synthetic and natural. Coats' Drima is an all-purpose synthetic thread for machining and hand sewing any fabric. It is on easily stored, slim plastic spools (which nevertheless take 100 yards) and is available in a comprehensive range of colours.

4. Pure silk, although expensive, is a soft elastic thread which works into woollen fabrics particularly well and is excellent for hand sewing. A wide range of colours is available, but it is not stocked by all haberdashery shops.

5. Machine embroidery thread (e.g. Anchor Machine Embroidery) is used for all types of decorative machining and for household darning done on the machine, but it also produces excellent results when used on sheer fabrics such as chiffon, lace, georgette and on silks. Use in place of tacking thread for tacking up fine fabric as the thread is fine and soft and will not harm the material. Machine embroidery thread is available in a wide range of colours in Nos. 30 and 50 and up to 100, but the thread is finer than other sewing threads bearing the same number.

6. Button thread—see *Buttons*.

TOP STITCHING

This is stitching normally done by machine used as a decorative feature. Tack and press the work well and mark a guide line with chalk or tacking or use the machine foot as a guide. The machine stitch should be slightly bigger than normal and with thick fabrics it may be necessary to loosen the top tension a little. Always work from the right side. For more conspicuous stitching buttonhole twist or fine crochet cotton may be used.

TRACE TACKING   See *Slip Tacking*

TUCKS

Tucks are stitched folds of fabric used mainly for decoration but sometimes put near the hems of children's clothes to be let down later, and in this case they are put in the garment last of all. Decorative tucks are made early on in the construction of the garment and they should run with the straight grain.

1. *Wide Tucks*

First cut a cardboard template exactly the width of the tucks. Mark with tacks exactly on the straight grain, the fold of the first tuck, beginning with the underneath one. Fold and tack the tuck. Press and machine this tuck, removing the tackings. Make the second tuck by measuring from the machine stitching and proceed as before. Do not press the tucks in the direction they have to go until all are complete.

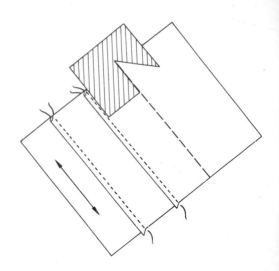

2. *Pin Tucks*

So called probably because they are only the width of a pin. They may be made by hand or using an automatic machine such as the Bernina Record. If a large area such as a yoke is to be tucked, then take a large piece of fabric, tuck it all over, press it and then lay on the pattern piece to cut out. Better results are often obtained by working them with the weft threads as there is a little give and it prevents puckering.

(*a*) BY HAND; Mark with tacks, exactly on the straight grain, the position of the first tuck. Fold the material on this line and tack about $\frac{1}{4}''$ (8 mm) back from the fold. Press and then machine very close to the fold, using a fine thread and needle. (They can, of course, be made by working a fine running stitch along the fold.) Remove the tacks, press the stitching and work the position of the next tuck by measuring from the machining and proceed as before.

(*b*) BY MACHINE. Place the fabric on tissue or typing paper. Use No. 50 or 60 machine embroidery and two needles in the machine. Fit the grooved tucking foot and proceed to machine the tucks. The thread in the spool pulls the two top threads together, so causing the fabric to rise. They are best worked fairly close; the tucks that have been worked run in adjacent grooves, so keeping following tucks perfectly straight. NOTE: It is essential to take great care to work the first tuck exactly on the straight grain.

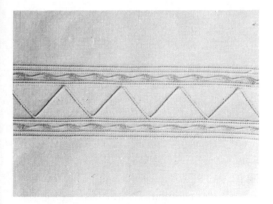

Pin tucks worked on a Bernina Record

3. *Corded or Raised Tucks*
Mark the position of the first tuck with tacks, and wrap the fabric around crochet cotton or cord and tack close to the cord. Machine either using the piping foot or work running stitches. Corded tucks may also be made on the machine using method 2, but threading crochet cotton from below up through the small round hole in the plate under the foot.

V

VELCRO See *Fasteners*

VELVET
Many velvets are now uncrushable and stain-resistant as well as water-repellent, but to obtain good results they still require careful handling.

1. Choose a simple style, preferably one designed especially for velvet. It should have few seams or buttonholes. If buttonholes are essential make either bound or machine-made ones, backing the area with a lightweight iron-on interfacing (e.g. Vilene F2).

2. Hold the fabric both ways to see which gives the richer effect, mark the top with chalk on the wrong side and cut all pieces in this direction.

3. If pile catches when folding, either cut singly from wrong side or place tissue paper between layers.

4. Use silk thread or synthetic thread (e.g. Coats' Drima), machine with twelve to fifteen stitches to 1″ (five and a half to seven to 1 cm), a small needle and hand-sewing needle No. 9–11.

5. Use needles in place of pins. Mark with tailor tacks, using machine embroidery thread, and use this for all tacking.

6. The fabric can be mounted on rayon taffeta or Jap silk if carefully done.

7. Use only open seams, carefully tacked with tissue paper between, and stitch the way of the pile.

8. Reduce the bulk as much as possible by trimming seams and splitting darts.

9. Neaten seams by overcasting or bind with strips of net.

10. Never over-fit.

11. Use organza or net as interfacing.

12. Put strips of net or organza in hemlines.

13. Fasten with an invisible zip (e.g. Alcozip) as this avoids any top stitching on the velvet.

14. To press, lay a strip of the fabric pile uppermost on the sleeve board, place the work pile downwards on this and press with a slightly damp muslin and warm to medium hot iron (depending on fibre). Only hold iron over muslin, never let go. Small parts such as darts may be pressed by standing the iron up, covering the base with damp muslin and holding the work against it.

VISCOSE RAYON

This fibre is made from cotton waste or wood-pulp, and is such a versatile fibre that it can be spun and woven to resemble many other fabrics made from other fibres, and this often causes uncertainty as to the origin. Examples of this are linen-look rayon, rayon sailcloth, brushed rayon, spun rayon, rayon dupion, slub rayon, rayon ottoman, rayon surah and shantung. It is also made into brocades, taffeta and furnishing rayons. Most of these fabrics fray easily but otherwise are not difficult to sew. They wash easily by hand or machine provided they are not allowed to become too soiled.

WAISTBAND

1. CUTTING. Cut the band *across* the selvedge, that is, with the weft threads, as the fabric has a small amount of give in this direction that makes for comfort. Cut the band allowing turnings and $1''-1\frac{1}{2}''$ (2·5–4 cm) underwrap as shown, and mark these allowances with chalk or tacks.

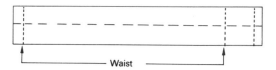

Waist

2. WIDTH. The width of the band varies according to style, personal taste, the fabric and method of finish, but wide bands wrinkle and may be uncomfortable during wear. One inch (2·5 cm) is a fairly good width. With thin fabrics, cut the band twice the finished width plus the width of two turnings.

To reduce bulk the inside may be made of lining and for this cut the band the finished width plus the width of two turnings and cut a piece of lining of the same size.

The inner edge of the band may be finished with straight seam binding to enable it to be sewn down more easily.

3. STIFFENING. Use petersham, petersham ribbon, belt-backing or heavyweight bonded interfacing of exactly the width of the finished waistband. Place it in position and herringbone to the fabric or attach with Bondina Fusible Fleece, cutting away the end turnings. If lining is being used for the inner part, stitch the stiffening to the centre of the band and then join the lining to it by stitching just off the edge of the interfacing. If attaching tape to the edge, machine it to the edge of the band.

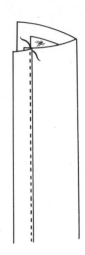

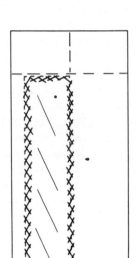

4. ATTACHING. A neat fastening is achieved by attaching the band with the edge level with the placket edge so that the other end forms an underwrap. If preferred the band can be applied so that it forms an overlap.

Place band to right side of skirt or slacks and machine on the fitting line. Turn in end turnings and herringbone along the lower edge of the underwrap. Fold band and tack the top fold, then fold under raw edge of band (or lining) and hem into machine stitches, slip-stitching the ends. Binding is hemmed into the machining.

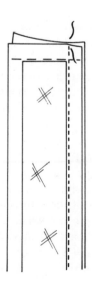

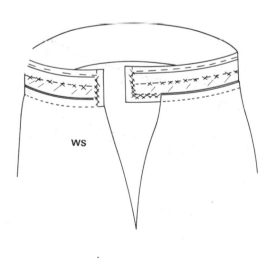

WS

5. FASTENERS. Sew a large eye to the end of the underwrap, then pin the band closed and sew a hook in position. Sew two large press studs to the end of the band; work a buttonhole in the end of the band and sew a button to correspond or attach a piece of Velcro.

WAISTLINE FINISHES

Hipster skirts and slacks and those which are not designed to fit the waist snugly do not require a waistband, and there are several methods of dealing with the waist which are very comfortable to wear. Suit skirts, too, are less bulky if made without a waistband.

1. FACING. This method may be used on mounted or unlined skirts and slacks. When seams and darts have been finished, cut and attach facings to fit the waistline. Cut them in fabric, or in lining if the fabric is thick. The curve of the waistline will be retained better if the turnings are trimmed but *not snipped*, and it helps to machine facings of lining to the turnings after attaching. Finish the facings by turning under and hemming each side of the zip and along the lower edge of the facing. If they are made from fabric then tack the lower edge flat and herringbone.

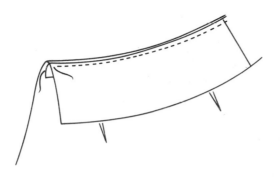

2. LINING FINISH. This is only for skirts and the loose lining is used for the finish. Make up the skirt, set in the zip and make up the lining. Place the right sides together, match up the darts and seams, and tack them together on the fitting line. Tack a piece of straight seam binding or tape on to the fitting line, to prevent stretching; after machining trim turnings, turn linings to the wrong side and finish with a row of machining worked from the right side.

3. INSIDE BAND OR PETERSHAM. These methods may be used on lined or unlined garments. Prepare the skirt by turning in the fitting line and working a row of machining close to the fold. Petersham: Cut a length of $\frac{3}{4}''$ (2 cm) petersham and hem or bind the ends. Sew two large hooks and eyes to the ends so that when fastened the petersham exactly fits the waist.

4. COVERED BAND: Cut a piece of heavyweight bonded interfacing about $\frac{3}{4}''$ (2 cm) wide equal in length to the waist measurement and cover it with lining as shown. Sew two large hooks and eyes in position to fasten. Pin the fastened band inside the skirt, tack in position and hem to the machine stitching.

WAISTLINE STAY

A dress with a waist join will fit better with a stay fixed inside and it is essential for any style with a bloused bodice.

When the dress is complete, cut a piece of petersham ribbon, hem or bind the ends and attach hooks as described under *Waistline Finishes*—Petersham. Pin this inside the waistline and hem on to the turnings, leaving about 1″ (2·5 cm) free under the dress opening.

WARP AND WEFT

The warp threads are those running down the fabric parallel with the selvedge. Garments should be cut with these threads running downwards to give a good hang. The warp threads are slightly stronger than the weft threads which run across the width of the fabric. The weft threads are inclined to stretch a little.

WEIGHTS

Lead weights of various sizes are used to improve the hang of various garments, particularly jackets, coats and long dresses. They have a hole through the centre for sewing them in position, but it is often best to enclose them in lining before attaching, especially if used with lightweight fabrics, for example where a single weight is used to hold in position the folds of a cowl or draped neckline.

WOOLLEN FABRICS

Woollen fibres are available in many different grades and they can be knitted, made into felt or knitting wool or woven into either woollens, the thicker hairy-surfaced woollen such as tweed, or the worsteds which are thin, often silky, with a smooth surface which shows up the pattern clearly. Types of weave include plain, hopsack or basket, dogstooth check, crêpe, bouclé, georgette, herringbone, face cloth, blazer cloth, double-faced or reversible cloth, flannel, as well as a vast range of novelty fabrics. Fabrics made from camel, mohair, vicuna, cashmere, alpaca often resemble wool and are sometimes mixed with wool, and are normally classified with wool for the purpose of sewing.

Woollen fabrics need lining as they are soft and tend to lose their shape. Some need mounting as well as lining. They are best sewn with mercerised thread or pure silk thread (which is slightly elastic), or with Coats' Drima. They are easy to sew provided careful attention is paid to the size of the machine stitch, to the use seams and edge finishes, and most of all to pressing. With adequate care and time spent, results can be achieved with good-quality wool which are second to none in dressmaking.

Y

YOKES

Yokes are usually made double, both for additional strength and because the inner layer of material can be used to neaten the joins. Use either two layers of fabric or a layer of fabric and a layer of lining fabric. (Choose a lining fabric that is suitable for the garment and one that will stand up to washing and ironing if the garment needs it.)

Place the back section of garment between two yoke pieces and machine. Press the join and then attach the other yoke edge to the other piece of garment and press. Use the edge of the

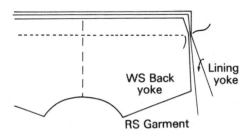

lining yoke to neaten the raw edges by hemming into the machine stitches.

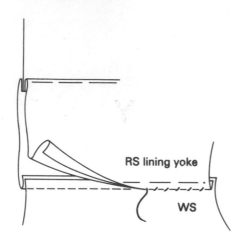

Yokes on dresses, skirts, etc., are constructed in the same way, using the lining to both strengthen and neaten.

Z

ZIPS

1. *Types*

The choice of zip lies between metal teeth, plain or coloured, on coloured cotton tape, coloured nylon spiral teeth on matching cotton tape, a jumbo zip with big brass or plastic coloured teeth on plain or fancy tape, and the zip which is invisible when closed as the teeth are turned inwards by the runner.

2. *Choice*

Choice of zip depends upon the style of garment, the type and weight of the fabric and the position of the zip opening. If correctly chosen and stitched and provided the zip is long enough it should not break during normal use. Coats, jackets, skirts, and slacks should have a strong,

fairly heavy type of zip whilst a nylon zip can be used on lightweight fabrics and knitwear.

3. *Method*

The method of insertion depends upon the thickness of the fabric and its weave, how much seam allowance is available and whether the garment is lined or not.

PREPARATION

In all cases the seam should be completed and the seam neatening worked for the whole length of the opening. In most cases the opening is

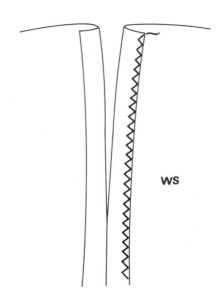

stitched up either with small tacks or with a large machine stitch. This is to ensure that the zip remains covered. Curved seams should be snipped. Complete all pressing before putting in the zip; never attempt more than a very light steaming after the zip has been put in. Remember never to put an iron directly on nylon teeth.

116

Try to manage without pins, but if this is not possible use only one at a time, putting it in horizontally and taking it right under the zip.

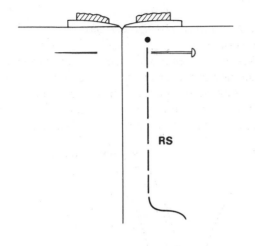

4. *Position of Zip in Seam*

Side placket or gap left in seam—leave the opening *exactly* the length of the zip teeth.

Back neck or skirt—place zip with slider slightly below the fitting line to allow facing, collar or band to be sewn on. After stitching, fold the ends of the tape to a horizontal position so that they are out of the way when the edge is finished.

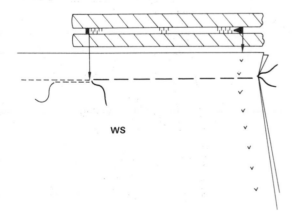

5. *Stitching*

Zips may be sewn in by hand or machine and the choice depends very much upon the thickness of the fabric, and also on the type of fabric and what equipment is available—for example, one-sided zip foot. If the zip is to be machined in, the stitching is best done from the outside, not the zip side. Using a fine thread and a stitch that is not too small (not less than twelve stitches to the inch (five and a half to 1 cm)). Best results are obtained by using a piping foot or a zip foot, obtainable as an attachment for most machines, as this enables the stitching to be done close to the teeth. If possible stitch both sides in the same direction, from top to bottom. With thick fabrics the machine foot compresses the fabric and tends to make a roll which lifts and reveals the zip, so either machine a little further away from the teeth or sew in by hand. To do this use single thread and work the stitch as shown, putting the needle back into the point where the thread emerges, so producing a row of dents but with no thread showing. Use a No. 8 or 9 Between needle and make the stitch as short as possible. For added strength the tapes may be hemmed to the turning allowance on the wrong side.

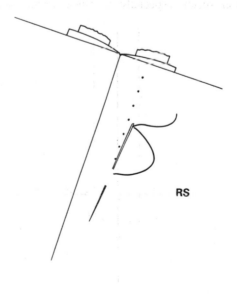

6. *The Slider*

The slider is wider than the teeth and there are two ways of stitching past it: either widen the machine stitching or pull the slider down a little way. To do this, first raise the machine foot but leave the needle in the work, move the slider, lower the foot and continue machining.

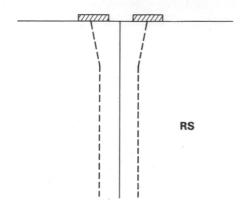

7. *The Lower End of the Zip*

The stitching of the seam should be well fastened off and may be strengthened with a bar tack. Stitch the sides of the zip first and either stitch across the bottom below the end stop or machine to a point. This second shape usually produces a flatter result, especially on thick fabrics. When

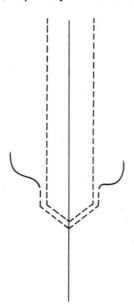

using the uneven hems method (see below) it may be best not to stitch across the bottom as this can produce a bulge. This will not leave a weak point, as with this method the strain is taken by the seam.

8. *Inserting Zips—Even Hems*
METHOD 1

Turn in the seam allowances on the fitting line, tack and press. Take care not to stretch it during pressing. If the fabric is thick and also mounted on a lining it may be advisable to trim the lining back to the fitting line first. Place the zip in

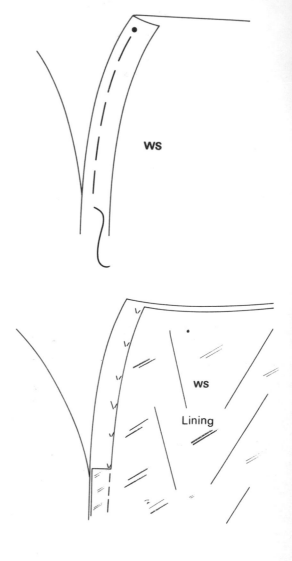

position so that the folded edge extends halfway over the teeth. Tack each side and then oversew the two folded edges together to prevent them being pulled off the zip during stitching. Machine or hand-stitch $\frac{1}{4}''$ (8 mm) from the centre folds. NOTE: Where checks have to be matched, tack and stitch one side, oversew the folds matching the checks, then tack and stitch the second side.

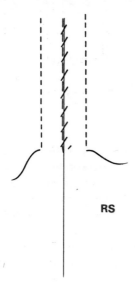

RS

METHOD 2

After stitching up the seam, stitch up the gap left for the zip, using a big machine stitch or small tackings. Press open right up to the top. Working from the wrong side, lay the zip right side down on to the seam and tack both sides, making sure that the teeth are over the join. Stitch in the zip; remove the big machine stitches.

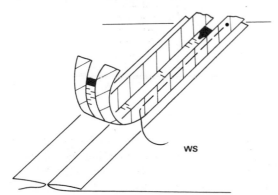

WS

Uneven Hems

Turnings of at least $1''$ (2·5 cm) are required.

METHOD 1

On the underside turn in the seam allowance $\frac{1}{8}''$ (4 mm) outside the fitting line (that is, nearer to the raw edge), tack and press the fold. Lay this fold on to the zip tape, pushing the fold close to the teeth, tack and machine working from top to bottom. Always sew this part by machine as it is difficult to sew strongly enough by hand, close to an edge. Snip the seam allowance at the lower end of the tape so that it will lie flat. Neaten the raw edges of this snip.

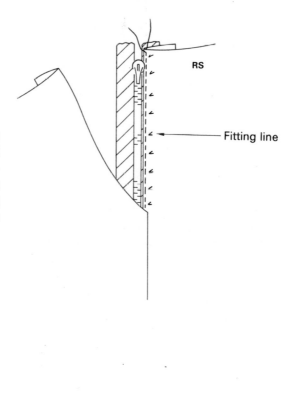

RS

Fitting line

Turn in the seam allowance on the second side, tack and press, and lay this right over the zip, matching the fitting lines. Hold the fold down with oversewing and then tack through fabric and tape close to the zip. Stitch by hand or machine.

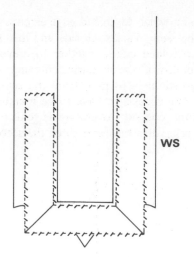

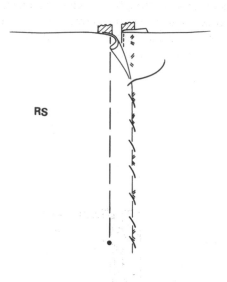

Measure the width of the zip teeth, fold back the garment turnings (or cut a slit and turn back), leaving a gap exactly equal to the width of the teeth, snip into the corners at the bottom and turn under the small triangle so formed. Neaten and strengthen the edges by hemming seam binding all round the opening. Tack the zip in position and machine close to the teeth. A second row of machining may be worked $\frac{1}{4}''$ (8 mm) away from this.

METHOD 2

Stitch up the seam, stitch up the gap left for the zip, press open the whole seam. Fold the underneath turning $\frac{1}{8}''$ (4 mm) from the stitching. Press the fold, lay it on the zip tape, and stitch as described in Method 1. Make sure that the zip and turning are lying flat, then tack and machine the second side.

NOTE: With both these methods the row of stitching which shows will be about $\frac{1}{2}''$ (15 mm) from the seam line.

Conspicuous Zips

This method is often used on knitted fabrics but also as a decorative feature—for example, jumbo zips. It is not necessary to have a seam.

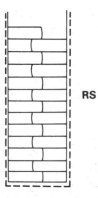

Invisible Alcozips

These are suitable for all fabrics but perhaps especially so for medium and heavyweight materials: for knitted fabrics where the material rolls naturally into position, and for lacy-weave fabrics in which an ordinary zip could easily be caught. They are perfect, too, in velvet and pile fabrics. The zip is invisible because the teeth are folded back out of sight by the runner as the zip closes, and the zip is stitched to the turnings only. Even the tapes will not show if the zip is correctly sewn in. Use the colour nearest to your fabric although it is not necessary to match it up exactly as with an ordinary zip fastener.

Invisible Alcozips may be sewn in equally well by hand or by machine, the preparation being slightly different from that of an ordinary zip.

PREPARATION OF SEAM

1. Mark off the length of seam to be left open for the zip by placing the zip beside the seam. Leave seam open to top of slider. Machine up the main part of the seam to this point and fasten off the stitching strongly. Remove tackings.

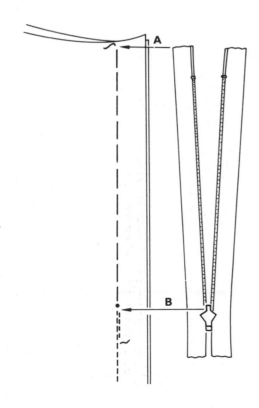

2. Close the remainder of the seam as shown, using either a very small tacking stitch or by using a big machine stitch.

3. Press open the whole seam very carefully, using a method of pressing suitable for the material (see *Pressing*). Careful pressing of the seam at this stage is vital because once the zip is in position it is impossible to press the fabric and a sharp crease along the fold will ensure that the tape will not be visible during wear. A curved seam should be snipped at intervals before being pressed.

TACKING THE ZIP IN POSITION

1. With the zip closed place the top tapes level with the raw edge of the material and with the teeth uppermost lay it centrally along the pressed seam. Tack the zip in position, using small tacking stitches and an occasional backstitch, *stitching the tape to the turning only*. Lift the turnings as little as possible and keep checking that the centre of the zip is still over the seam.

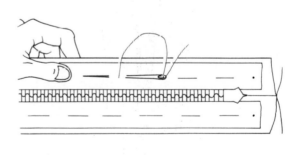

2. Unpick the stitches which hold the opening together, taking care not to move the zip from its tacked position.

STITCHING—BY MACHINE

1. Open the zip fully and flatten out the teeth a little with the fingers. With a zip foot or piping foot on the machine, stitch the first side, starting at the top and stopping when the slider is reached; reverse the stitching for 1″ (2·5 cm) to fasten off firmly. The machine stitches should be about $\frac{1}{16}$″ (2 mm) away from the teeth, this is about as close as it is possible to stitch.

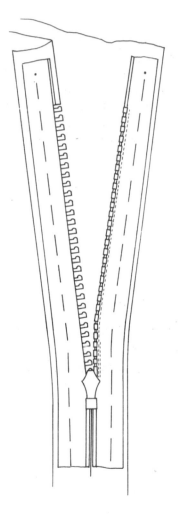

2. Adjust the zip foot and stitch the second side in the same way, again starting at the top. Cut off the machine ends to prevent them being caught in the zip.

Stitching in an Alcozip by machine

3. Close the zip a little way and then work a short row of machining to attach the bottom few inches of tape to the turnings. Make sure the two rows overlap a little as shown. This short row of stitching will be a little further from the teeth than the first row.

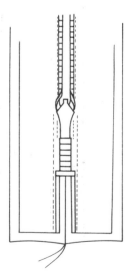

4. At the top, fold back the tapes and secure to the turnings with a few stitches. The facing, waistband, collar, etc., is now attached to the fitting line in the usual way.

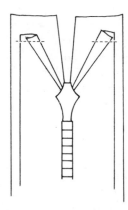

STITCHING—BY HAND

This zip may be sewn in very well by hand, using a small strong backstitch worked as close as possible to the teeth. Although this should prove secure it is possible to work a row of machining along the edge of the tape as an added security.

After sewing in, remove all tackings and fasten all ends of thread, and then open and close zip gently once or twice to allow the teeth to curl over into position. Never press after the zip is in.

INVISIBLE ALCOZIPS IN LIGHTWEIGHT FABRICS

Before inserting the zip, place a strip of lightweight interfacing (organdie or lawn), about 2″ (5 cm) wide, on the wrong side of the work at each side of the opening. Baste them in position and then proceed to insert the zip in the usual way.

SHORT REFERENCE INDEX